"Puppies go through all the stages their human counterparts do—at startling speed. What makes Ms. Randolph's book so important is that it helps you recover fast enough to face the next stage. Bravo!"

Roger Caras, author of
The Roger Caras Dog Book and
A Celebration of Dogs

"A valuable reference, one that will be used over and over again in the first few months a home is shared with a dog."

The Chattanooga Times

"Offers much needed guidance for pet owners, and Randolph's understanding analysis of common problems provides good suggestions. . . . Unique."

Library Journal

By Elizabeth Randolph:

YOUR PET'S COMPLETE RECORD BOOK
HOW TO BE YOUR CAT'S BEST FRIEND*
THE COMPLETE BOOK OF DOG HEALTH
(with The Animal Medical Center)
THE COMPLETE BOOK OF CAT HEALTH
(with The Animal Medical Center)
HOW TO HELP YOUR PUPPY GROW UP TO BE A
   WONDERFUL DOG*
THE BASIC BIRD BOOK*
(with Douglas G. Aspros, DVM)
THE BASIC BOOK OF FISH KEEPING*
RABBITS AND OTHER FURRY PETS*

Published by Fawcett Books

Books published by The Ballantine Publishing Group are available at quantity discounts on bulk purchases for premium, educational, fund-raising, and special sales use. For details, please call 1-800-733-3000.

HOW TO HELP YOUR PUPPY GROW UP TO BE A WONDERFUL DOG

Elizabeth Randolph
**with Animal Behavior Consultant
Dr. Ginger Hamilton**

FAWCETT CREST • NEW YORK

A Fawcett Crest Book
Published by Ballantine Books
Copyright © 1987 by Elizabeth Randolph

http://www.randomhouse.com

Library of Congress Catalog Card Number: 86-21848

ISBN 0-345-47277-2

Cover photo © Walter Chandoha 1987

This edition published by arrangement with Macmillan Publishing Company, a division of Macmillan, Inc.

Manufactured in the United States of America

For PHOEBE,
a pretty Wonderful Dog!

CONTENTS

*Each bold-faced entry is a self-contained, in-depth Detailed Discussion of
one aspect of puppy management or behavior that may be applicable at many
stages of a puppy's life.

ACKNOWLEDGMENTS

I would especially like to thank Dr. Ginger Hamilton for sharing with me her invaluable professional insights into canine behavior and management.

For help in obtaining background materials, my thanks to Tim Donovan, Public Information Division of the American Veterinary Medical Association (AVMA).

Thanks to Joan R. Heilman for her original suggestion from which this book developed.

Thank you also to Arlene Friedman, who was my Editorial Director at Macmillan, and her associate, Emily Easton.

And as always, thank you to my husband, Arthur Hettich, for his continuing support and encouragement.

ELIZABETH RANDOLPH

PREFACE:
WHAT THIS BOOK IS ABOUT

Dog pounds and animal shelters are full of half-grown and young-adult dogs that are no longer wanted by their owners. Why? Those who have studied the problem have discovered that many of these dogs are given away because they did not live up to their owners' expectations in one way or another. There are probably several reasons for this: an uninformed initial choice of a puppy, a lack of knowledge about a growing puppy's physical needs, and a poor understanding of how to handle a puppy. Result: an unhappy marriage of owner and dog.

The decision to own a puppy should be based on more than whim. Choosing a pet that will probably spend at least ten years in your household should be fun, interesting, and exciting, but not impulsive. In the first part of this book there are some guidelines to help you make an intelligent, thoughtful choice.

Common sense should tell you that, contrary to what some would like you to believe, puppy ownership is not a continuous pleasure and delight. Mixed in with the fun is hard work, sacrifice, upset, and annoyance: trips to the veterinarian; walks in the snow and rain; spills, "mistakes,'' and hair to be cleaned up; favorite objects chewed or broken, and so forth. Even experienced dog owners sometimes tend to forget just how much time and effort proper puppy care can take. To most people it is well worth it to see a small puppy grow into a beautiful, responsive, companionable dog. However, if you and your family are not prepared for the responsibility and care that puppy ownership entails, you should not consider it.

A great many books have been written to help parents understand the development of a child—the various stages of physical change and those of social/behavioral upheaval and calm. Most aim both to reassure parents that their children are ''normal'' and to give them tools so that they can work with their children's natural development in a positive way.

This book will do the same thing for puppy owners. It is not a dog training book or one that purports to contain a magic formula to make all dogs good. It is about the normal development of most puppies: how they grow, what their physical and social needs are at various stages, when they are ready to learn specific types of behavior, and what the optimum time is to anticipate a possible behavior problem and nip it in the bud before it becomes a bad habit. Noted animal psychologist Dr. Ginger Hamilton has contributed her professional expertise to provide material on all the aspects of puppy behavior that are covered. The overview chapter about puppy behavior contains some never-before-published findings about how your own temperament can affect your puppy's behavior, and there are also twenty-seven sections (*Detailed Discussions*) throughout the book dealing with specific aspects of puppy behavior and management at the appropriate stages in a puppy's development. These *Detailed Discussions* are designed to help you offset or at least mitigate future behavior problems.

Even the happiest and most successful dog owners often

put up with less-than-ideal behavior on the part of their pets, just as parents do with their children. This book will enable you to understand better what's going on at each step of your puppy's short journey from helpless infant to independent adult. From a human standpoint this journey is compressed into a very short period of time—only twelve to eighteen months, depending on the size and breed of dog, compared to between fifteen to twenty years in a person's life. The book outlines the stages of a puppy's development and suggests commonsense ways for you to work within this development in positive ways that help your puppy grow up to be a responsive, enjoyable, satisfactory pet that will fit into your household and life-style and give years of pleasure—in other words, to grow up to be a wonderful dog.

Happy puppy ownership!

ELIZABETH RANDOLPH

PART ONE

Planning Ahead

1

A Serious Decision—
What Do You Want
in a Dog?

No one consciously sets out to acquire a puppy in order to give it up after a few months or a year, but many people end up doing just that because they fail to realize that there is a lot more to dog ownership than simply feeding and walking. It may be trite but it bears repeating here that a puppy is not a wind-up toy that can be simply put aside when you tire of playing with it; it is a living creature that requires a lot of daily care and considerable love and attention.

Before you consider getting a puppy, ask yourself some questions: Are you willing and able to take proper care of a puppy? Why do you want a puppy? What do you want that puppy to be like?

Are You Willing and Able to Take Proper Care of a Puppy?

Before you answer yes too quickly, think about these things:

- Puppies require a lot of human interaction and care. Very young puppies (up to three or four months old) should not be left completely alone for long. If all human family members are going to be out most of every day, there are a couple of solutions to this problem: Arrangements can be made for somebody to come in and take care of the puppy at least once during the day; two puppies can be obtained at the same time, or an older companion animal can provide companionship (see *Another Pet for Company?* page 250).

- A puppy will form firm attachments to its family during the first few months of life. Extended owner absences can prevent this; therefore, for at least the first four or five months you should put off long business trips or family vacations that do not include the puppy. This may be difficult.

- Early experiences and interactions with people play a large role in the development of a puppy. In addition to taking care of a puppy's physical needs, you should plan to spend one or more hours each day in short play sessions, no matter how tired or busy you are.

- Good and bad habits and behaviors begin young. If you want your pet to develop into a well-behaved adult dog, you have to spend time working with it to develop good habits.

- Until they are one year old, puppies require frequent visits to the veterinarian (every two to four weeks) for immunizations. This takes time and money.

- Dogs need regular brushing and/or combing by their owners, and some breeds require professional grooming. These routines should be started as early as possible so that the puppy becomes accustomed to them.

- No matter how careful you are or how well behaved your

puppy is, there will invariably be "accidents" in the house. Rugs will be soiled, things will be knocked over or chewed, and hair may be shed.

In short, puppy ownership involves an investment of energy, time, patience, and money, and almost surely entails some household upsets. Unless you recognize these things ahead of time and are willing to accept them as a normal part of puppy ownership, you should not consider getting a puppy.

A word should be said here about children and puppy care. It is often bemoaned that no matter how many promises children make ahead of time about puppy care, the adults always end up doing the lion's share of the work. Common sense should come to bear here. It is all very well for an eight-year-old to promise to take care of every aspect of a puppy's care, but it is hardly realistic and not entirely practical to expect him to be able to do this. Parents should remember that all children occasionally become involved in play with friends and forget their responsibilities. What's more, a child cannot feed or walk a puppy when he's in school or bed, for instance, nor can he usually manage to take the puppy to the veterinarian or groomer. A reasonable plan in which all family members share in the various puppy-care tasks usually works best and prevents tears, guilt, and aggravation, to say nothing of potential neglect of the puppy. This will be discussed in more detail under *Who Will Do What?*, page 36.

Why Do You Want a Dog?

This may seem like another obvious question, but it is not as simple as it appears. Leaving aside specialized reasons for dog ownership, such as hunting or other sports, breeding for profit, guarding or working, which we will not deal with in this book, there are many diverse reasons why an individual or family may think they want a pet dog: for companionship and affection, as a playmate for children, for protection of people or property, to teach children responsibility, because it would be fun, or to keep up with neighbors and friends. In a family, each member may have a different reason or a combination of reasons for wanting a dog.

It is also a good idea to consider the fact that family circumstances will almost certainly change during the life span of the average dog: The children for whom a puppy is chosen as a playmate will grow up and move away; perhaps the home it was chosen to protect may be exchanged for a city apartment; and other changes in family makeup and life-style may occur. Although it is impossible to predict all the possible changes that may take place in your family during a dog's lifetime, you should be aware that your initial reasons for getting a puppy may not be valid in a few years and a dog may not fit into your life-style then. Sometimes when these factors are carefully examined it turns out that dog ownership is not a wise decision.

What Do You Want Your Dog to Be Like?

If you and your family have decided that you do want a dog and are ready to take on the responsibility of puppy ownership, do you have any idea what kind of dog you want? This is the time to think a lot about this question because your choice has a great deal to do with your ultimate satisfaction with your pet.

What is each family member's ideal dog? Does it have long or short hair? Is it soft and silky, or rough to the touch? Are the ears long and floppy, or upright? Nose pointy, round, or pushed in? How big is it—a lap dog or a giant? What about behavior? If a shy child or quiet couple wants a sweet, cuddly, soft, unexcitable dog, they would be extremely unhappy with a bouncy, energetic, hard-coated terrier. On the other hand, a delicate toy would be extremely disappointing to a family of energetic children who are hoping for a tireless playmate. Is there a particular breed or type of dog you used to know or someone else owns that you think of as an ideal pet?

Each family member should write down his or her preferences, and the family should then compare notes. If all agree on a particular breed or type of dog, the job is much easier, but even without universal agreement a compromise can usually be reached as long as each person has a say. See Table I: Sample Preference Chart for Choosing a Companion Puppy, on the following page.

There are usually several breeds or types of dogs that fit the description you have come up with, and now the research should begin to find the "ideal" dog for you. Although a mixed-breed puppy may well suit your family's perfect-pet profile, the characteristics of purebred dogs are more readily predictable, so we will stick to them in our discussion.

Each family member should participate in the research; even very young children can look through library books at pictures of dog breeds. Go to dog shows, talk to breeders and owners, and read all you can about the breeds or types of dog you are considering. Bear in mind that most breeders are not entirely objective about their breeds, so it pays to talk to as many owners as possible in order to find out if there are any particular drawbacks or problems with a given breed of dog. Remember that what is acceptable to some people may not be to you. Devotees of a particular breed of dog may feel that its good characteristics far outweigh the bad, but you may not feel that way.

Table 1 *Sample Preference Chart
for Choosing a Companion Puppy*

Physical Characteristics

Size (for example: Giant, Large, Medium, Small, Toy): _____
Color: _____
Coat type: _____
   Importance of ease of care, lack of shedding: _____
Ears: _____
Tail: _____
Nose: _____
Eyes: _____
Physical stamina (for example: hardy and sturdy; delicate and sensitive.
   Primarily an outdoors or indoors dog?): _____

Behavior/Temperament

Calm, not very active: Indoors: _____ Outdoors: _____
Very active: Indoors: _____ Outdoors: _____
Gentle, cuddly: _____
Rough, vigorous: _____
Playful: _____
Quiet, rarely barks: _____
Outgoing, friendly, sociable with everyone: _____
"One-man (family) dog," reserved with strangers: _____
Importance of (that is: very, somewhat, not particularly): _____
   Obedience level: _____
   Learning ability: _____
   Watchdog ability: _____
Other important qualities: _____

What follows are some general characteristics you may
want to take into account when choosing a dog.

Characteristics to Consider

In the course of your research into kinds of dogs you
may come across references to "overbreeding" or some
similar term in discussions of certain breeds. Or you may
hear statements such as: "All such-and-such dogs are un-
trustworthy" (or "hard to housebreak" or "snappish" or

Table 2 *Some Examples of Breeds with Life Expectancies That Are Longer or Shorter than Average*

Longer than Average (fifteen to twenty years):
Most of the toy breeds, and many very small dogs; Boston terrier; Doberman pinscher; fox terrier; Irish setter; Kerry blue terrier; schipperke; standard schnauzer; Welsh corgi (Cardigan and Pembroke); West Highland white terrier; whippet

Shorter than Average (under ten years):
Boxer; bulldog (English bulldog); many very large breeds such as Saint Bernard, Great Pyrenees, and Newfoundland; and all of the giant breeds, in particular Great Dane, Irish wolfhound, Scottish deerhound

---

"sickly"). It is wise to consider the source of this kind of remark since the information is often based on second- or third-hand knowledge or on the acquaintance of only one dog.

However, certain breeds or types of dogs may have a predisposition toward some potentially unpleasant physical or behavioral characteristics. Some of these seemingly unimportant characteristics, such as snoring and drooling, may be extremely annoying to some people, but breeders seldom bring them up if you don't ask about them.

More important, certain breeds and types of dog do have predispositions toward potentially serious physical and behavioral disorders that you should know about. Nothing is sadder than finding out that the adorable puppy you've already grown to love has developed a serious physical problem or an unacceptable behavior trait. (For more information about some of these predispositions, see *Choosing a Source*, page 22, and *Choosing a Puppy*, page 41.)

What follows is not designed to scare you away from a particular breed or type of dog but is meant only to make you into an intelligent consumer.

LIFE EXPECTANCY

One characteristic that many inexperienced dog owners completely fail to consider is life span. It is generally assumed that a healthy, well-cared-for pet dog will live an average of twelve to fifteen years; but there are a number of breeds that have longer-than-average life expectancies and others that are unfortunately quite short-lived. Although this may not be a factor for many people, others may want to consider a puppy's expected life span when they choose a pet. The table above lists some of the breeds that are normally either above or below the average in expected life span.

Physical Characteristics

There are also a number of general physical characteristics that may affect your decision. Purebred dogs are divided by the American Kennel Club (AKC) into certain classifications or "groups": sporting dogs, hounds, working dogs, terriers, toys and non-sporting dogs. These groups divide dogs by their functions—what they were bred to *do*—rather than by their physical characteristics. Except in the case of the toys, which are grouped by size, there is usually no universal set of physical characteristics in any of these groups. In the hound group, for instance, you'll find little short-legged dachshunds, giant Irish wolfhounds, and delicate whippets. Haircoats can vary within a group from the sleek, smooth coat of a Weimaraner to the soft, silky coat of a golden retriever—both members of the sporting dogs group. So, for the purposes of choosing physical appearance, these groups have little bearing.

Table 3 *Approximate Average Size Classifications*

	Weight (pounds)	Height (inches)
Toys*	Up to 12	Up to 12
Small	10 to 30	9 to 17
Medium	20 to 65	11 to 25
Large	50 to 115	15 to 30
Giant	95 to 150+	28 to 32+

SIZE

Size should be thought of in terms of mass (the combination of height and weight) rather than simply height and/or weight. Other factors that combine to make a dog seem large or small are whether it is long-bodied or compact, slim or sturdy, long- or short-legged, and long- or short-tailed. As far as ease of handling and appropriateness for small spaces goes, prospective owners should also consider a dog's activity level and exercise requirements. See Table 3 for average weights and heights of dogs in various size categories.

HAIRCOAT

The amount of care a dog's coat requires, and its degree of shedding, is of primary concern to some people. Although all dogs need regular grooming (brushing and/or combing), some have coats that require daily care while others are comparatively easy to keep clean and neat with only weekly attention by their owners. Most of the breeds that must be professionally groomed need little additional maintenance from their owners.

Much depends on your own preference, the amount of time you have to spend on grooming, the amount of money you are willing and able to spend on professional grooming, and the degree of importance you place on a hair-free

* Some heavier and taller, especially males.

home. Of course, if there is an allergic person in the household, particular care must be taken to choose a dog that sheds very little or one that has been found to be relatively hypoallergenic due to its small amount of dander (the dandrufflike dry skin that is shed by all animals to a certain degree). There is some difference of opinion as to just which breeds fall into this category, but poodles and schnauzers are usually considered to be the most dander-free.

Dog coat types fall roughly into these general categories: smooth-coated, double-coated, wirehaired, long-haired, and curly-haired. They can further be divided into heavy year-round shedders, heavy seasonal shedders, normal year-round shedders, and minimum shedders (all dogs, even the so-called shedless breeds, must shed in order to replace old hair with new).

Some haircoat generalizations: Wirehaired and curly-haired dogs shed less than smooth-coated dogs. Double-coated dogs shed a great deal, and many, especially those with very heavy winter coats, lose their entire undercoats in the spring (this is often referred to as "blowing" a coat). Owners often have these dogs' coats professionally "pulled," or plucked at this time in order to get rid of the bulk of shed hair. Many water dogs have an oily coating on their fur to insulate them from moisture (Labradors, for instance). This oily coating can rub off and eventually leave a stain on furniture and walls. The size and color of a dog also affects how much it seems to shed. Obviously, white hair shows up on dark furniture and rugs, dark hair is more noticeable on light furnishings, and a big dog's fur is more voluminous than that of a smaller breed.

A generalized summary of coat care requirements and degree of shedding for some breeds are in Table 4.

EARS

The conformation of a dog's ears is not usually a major consideration in the degree of care required. You should know, however, that pendulous ears are apt to be more susceptible to traumatic injury than upright ears. Floppy ears can also prevent air circulation, which may lead to bacterial infection, and dogs with very hairy ears may develop hair plugs in their ears. Some breeds (Great Danes and Dobermans, for example) may have had their ears cropped by the breeder before adoption. This cosmetic surgery, designed to make a dog's ears stand upright, involves a lot of post-operative care by an owner in order to prevent infection.

FACE

Certain breeds of dog have been bred with very pushed-in noses and protruberant eyes. These dogs, known as brachycephalic breeds, are prone to serious nasal and eye problems. Boston terriers, boxers, bulldogs, Lhasa apsos, Pekingese, and pugs, for example, are subject to eye damage and disease because their eyes are not set very deeply in their sockets and are not well protected by lids.

On the less serious but possibly annoying side, pug-nosed breeds are almost always snorers and snorters, and are also apt to suffer from excessive flatulence because they regularly swallow a great deal of air.

Dogs with loose, pendulous lower lips, such as bloodhounds, boxers, Saint Bernards, Newfoundlands, mastiffs, and Great Pyrenees, tend to drool a lot.

13

Table 4   *Coat Care and Shedding
of Some Representative Breeds*

Amount of Care

Require regular professional care:
  Grooming and clipping—approximately every six weeks: poodle
  Pulling, trimming, and stripping—two to three times a year: most
  wirehaired terriers, Bedlington terriers, schnauzers
  "Pulling," or plucking—annual or semiannual: seasonal shedders
  (see below)

Require maximum (daily) care:
  All of the breeds with long, silky coats
  Afghan, bichon frise, collie (rough-coated), Dandie Dinmont, kees-
  hond, Lhasa apso, Maltese, Old English sheepdog, papillon, Pekingese, Pomeranian, Shetland sheepdog, Shih Tzu, silky terrier, Skye
  terrier, Yorkshire terrier

Especially easy coat care:
  Most short, sleek, smooth-coated breeds
  Affenpinscher, basenji,* Border terrier, Boston terrier,* boxer, bull-
  dog, Chihuahua, Dalmatian, Doberman pinscher, foxhounds, Great
  Dane, greyhounds,* Manchester terriers,* Norfolk and Norwich ter-
  riers, Labrador retriever, pointers, pug, Rhodesian ridgeback, sa-
  luki,* schnauzers,* schipperke, smooth-coated collie and dachshund,
  Welsh corgis, whippet*

Degree of Shedding

Very heavy shedders:
  Most double-coated breeds, including: chow chow, German shepherd, Pomeranian, Siberian husky

Heavy seasonal or once-a-year shedders:
  Akita, Alaskan malamute, chow chow, collie, Great Pyrenees, kees-
  hond, Newfoundland, Samoyed, Shetland sheepdog, Siberian husky

Little (if any) shedding:
  Most wirehaired dogs shed very little
  Basenji, bearded collie, Irish water spaniel, Maltese, poodles,
  schnauzers, Sealyham terrier, whippet, Yorkshire terrier

* Very clean, neat, and odorless.

PHYSICAL STAMINA/DELICACY

Sporting and working dogs, and most of the hounds and terriers, are generally hardy and able to withstand extremes of temperature well. Exceptions in the working dog category are boxers and Great Danes, both of which are sensitive to damp and cold. Among the hounds, greyhounds and whippets require protection from the cold. Almost all toys must be protected against temperature extremes, especially very cold weather.

Brachycephalic breeds are especially sensitive to the heat. Bulldogs and pugs, for example, frequently fall victim to heat exhaustion. Some double-coated breeds, such as the chow chow, are also very sensitive to extreme heat.

Temperament/Behavior Characteristics

Behavioral characteristics, as opposed to physical characteristics, can be determined to a certain extent by the group classification a particular dog breed falls into. As we mentioned before, this is because the groups are divided by purpose or function.

Large sporting dogs and hounds, for example, have been developed over the years to have a great deal of physical energy. That means that they require a lot of daily outdoor exercise in order to stay in top shape, both physically and emotionally. Thus, bloodhounds, foxhounds, Irish wolfhounds, pointers, retrievers, Scottish deerhounds, setters, and Weimaraners, for example, are not really suited to life in a city apartment. They are usually willing learners but need to be taught what is expected of them.

Working dogs are also generally physically active and strong and need a lot of vigorous daily exercise in order to remain happy. The larger working breeds (such as Alaskan malamute, Bouvier des Flandres, briard, bullmastiff,

15

Great Pyrenees, and Old English sheepdog) are not particularly suitable for urban life. Usually very intelligent and responsive to human demands, working dogs are apt to be somewhat strong-willed and stubborn, and even the smallest of them (the corgis and Shetland sheepdogs) require a firm hand.

Terriers, too, are energetic and vigorous, but because of their relatively small size, they usually can get enough exercise, even in the city. The males, in particular, tend to be very territorial and stubborn, and care must be taken to teach them early in life that territorial aggression and excessive barking are not acceptable.

Outdoor exercise requirements need to be differentiated from indoor activity level. A tiny Yorkshire terrier really does not require long runs for exercise (even though it still needs to be taken outdoors for social exposure and to relieve boredom), but owners of these little dogs know that they spend a great deal of time running around the house, inspecting and tending to things. If you want a dog that is calm indoors, some of the larger and giant breeds, such as bulldogs, basset hounds, Newfoundlands, mastiffs, Great Danes, Great Pyrenees, Irish wolfhounds, standard poodles, and even Scottish deerhounds, are surprisingly inactive in the house, provided they get enough daily outdoor exercise. Clumber spaniels are well known for their somewhat phlegmatic natures.

TEMPERAMENT

Temperament can vary widely in individual puppies; genetics, early handling, conditioning, and a number of unique characteristics all affect the ultimate individual ''personality'' of a dog.

Some breeds almost always seem to be born friendly, and others appear to be congenitally aloof or warm up only with immediate family—often referred to as a "one-man dog."

Generalizations about this aspect of a particular breed's temperament are necessarily subjective and are always subject to exceptions. In addition, there are, unfortunately, examples of some breeds that have been spoiled by careless breeding (see *Choosing a Puppy*, page 41). Most family dogs are good with considerate children and the children with whom they grow up. Many of the large and giant breeds must be carefully watched around small children, however, simply because of their size and strength.

WATCHDOG ABILITY

Almost every dog barks at particularly threatening noises. Some will bark only at strange animals when they approach their property, and others at unknown humans. Very territorial dogs (many terriers and some toys) bark at every sound. Many of the working dogs have been bred to guard livestock and/or property, and they possess above-average natural watchdog instincts. Very large dogs serve as useful watchdogs even when they are not especially territorial or aggressive. Their size alone serves as a deterrent to strangers.

You must be careful not to foster overaggressiveness or territoriality, especially in a dog that already is naturally protective. Needless to say, overly aggressive or territorial behavior that can be tolerated in a small dog or a toy cannot be allowed in a larger dog. Inexperienced owners should be extremely careful not to bite off more than they are able to chew when it comes to a large, powerful dog.

Even the most ingrained behavioral characteristics can be controlled or modified if an owner is willing and able to spend the time and knows how to do it. Table 5, which shows how certain breeds are apt to behave, may help the uninitiated to make an intelligent decision about what kind of dog to get.

Table 5 *Common Behavior and Temperamental Traits, and Some Breeds That Often Exhibit Them*

Trait	Examples of Breeds
Noise Level	
Especially quiet	Alaskan malamute, basenji, borzoi, papillon, whippet
Especially noisy— possibly excessive barking	Most of the terriers and many toys may bark excessively. Also cocker spaniel, dachshunds, Norwegian elkhound, retrievers, Shetland sheepdog, Weimaraner, Welsh corgis
Apt to bay/howl	All of the hounds (except the basenji), especially bassets and beagles, plus Alaskan malamute and Siberian husky
Activity Level	
Apt to roam	Most of the hounds plus American water and Brittany spaniels, collies, Great Pyrenees, Labrador retriever (male), pointers (mostly male), setters
Very active indoors	Most toys and many terriers, plus Alaskan malamute, basenji, bichon frise, corgis, dachshunds, Weimaraner
Very calm indoors	Most giant and large breeds provided they have plenty of outdoor exercise. Basset hound, Boston terrier, clumber spaniel, greyhound, Pekingese, pug, saluki, standard poodle, whippet

Table 5 *Common Behavior and Temperamental Traits, and Some Breeds That Often Exhibit Them (Cont.)*

Trait	Examples of Breeds
Sociability Level	
Aggressive to other dogs	Many of the breeds developed to chase prey. American Staffordshire terrier, akita, Alaskan malamute, Bedlington terrier, the Belgians, Border terrier, borzoi, boxer, Bouvier des Flandres, bulldog, bullmastiff, bull terrier, chow chow, corgis, fox terrier, giant schnauzer, Gordon setter, Irish terrier, Irish water spaniel, Kerry blue terrier, Norwegian elkhound, otter hound, Staffordshire bull terrier, Welsh terrier
Aloof with people	Chihuahua, chow chow, Scottish terrier, Vizsla
One-person or one-family dogs	Afghan, airedale, basenji, beagle, the Belgians, Bernese mountain dog, briard, Brittany spaniel, Cairn terrier, clumber spaniel, curly-coated retriever, dalmatian, Doberman pinscher, English springer spaniel, Gordon setter, Irish water spaniel, Irish wolfhound, keeshond, komander, Lhasa apso, Norwegian elkhound, Rhodesian ridgeback, rottweiler, Scottish deerhound, whippet
Outgoing, friendly	Affenpinscher, Alaskan malamute, basset hound, bearded collie, Bichon Frise, Boston terrier, Border terrier, boxer, Chesapeake Bay, flat-coated, golden and Labrador retrievers, cocker spaniel,* collie,* English setters, miniature schnauzer,* Newfoundland, Norfolk, and Norwich terriers, Old English sheepdog,* Samoyed, Shih Tzu, standard poodle, Welsh terrier, West Highland white terrier, Yorkshire terrier

* If unspoiled by poor breeding.

Table 5 *Common Behavior and Temperamental Traits, and Some Breeds That Often Exhibit Them (Cont.)*

Trait	Examples of Breeds
Natural watchdogs	All of the terriers and most of the working guard dogs, including akita, beagle, Brittany spaniel, the Belgians, Bouvier des Flandres, briard, Brussels griffon, collie, corgis, German shepherd, giant and standard schnauzers, Norwegian elkhound, Lhasa apso, otter hound, puli, Rhodesian ridgeback, Shetland sheepdog, Scottish deerhound

2

Getting Ready
for a Puppy

Now that you and your family have decided that you want
a puppy and have a good idea of what kind, you have to
get ready for the adoption.

Step one is to determine from whom you will obtain
your puppy. Then you should decide what veterinarian
you and your puppy will go to. (These steps may be re-
versed because you might want to use a veterinarian as
a source for a good puppy breeder.) Third, you and your
family need to make some initial decisions about space
management: where your pup will spend its first night in
your house and where it will stay during the day when it
is alone. It should be the same place if possible. You
should also figure out what you will need in the way of
equipment for the puppy's care, safety, and comfort. At
the same time, give some advance thought to the division
of puppy-care tasks—who will be responsible for feeding, cleaning up, grooming, and training. Last, but certainly not least, try to come to agreement about the basics
of puppy behavior that your family will stick to so that
the puppy won't be confused by contradictory messages.

As we emphasize throughout this book, early experiences can be either positive or negative learning episodes for a puppy. The kind of dog it grows up to be will be a measure of how well these early experiences are handled.

Choosing a Source

There are several reasons why it is important to choose your source carefully when you want a purebred puppy. No matter how conscientiously you raise a puppy, genetics will affect its ultimate physical health and emotional stability. Early handling—socialization by the breeder before you take over ownership—also affects a puppy's disposition. Although physical defects and behavioral quirks in a puppy can eventually be controlled or modified, they make your job much more difficult, and there is no reason why that should happen.

HEREDITARY PHYSICAL DISORDERS

Purebred dogs have been selectively bred over the years to enhance certain physical attributes. Unfortunately, this same selective breeding sometimes exacerbates undesirable physical traits. It is important for prospective puppy owners to know that some breeds have predispositions toward certain physical disorders. These disorders do not necessarily appear in a puppy's parents (sire and dam) but may have been passed along to a puppy in genes inherited from one or more of its grandparents or even great-grandparents.(These are known as recessive genes.) Table 6 lists some of the hereditary physical faults or predispositions that are known to occur in certain dog breeds.

Table 6 *Some Dog Breeds That Have Predispositions*
Toward Hereditary Physical Disorders

Autoimmune Disease

Systemic lupus erythematosus	German shepherd, Shetland sheepdog

Bleeding Disorder

Von Willebrand's disease (congenital)	Doberman pinscher

Deafness (congenital) Dalmatian

Digestive Problem

Pancreatic insufficiency	German shepherd

Endocrine Diseases

Cushing's syndrome (develops in middle to old age)	Boston terrier, boxer, dachshunds, poodles
Diabetes (develops in middle to old age)	Poodles (high incidence)
Juvenile onset (congenital)	Keeshond, golden retriever
Hyperthyroidism	Doberman pinscher, Great Dane, golden retriever, Irish setter

Eye Disorders

Optic nerve improperly formed at birth	Collie
Pannus	German shepherd
Retina improperly formed at birth	English springer spaniel, Labrador retriever
Retinal abnormality (surfaces later in life)	Cocker spaniel, collie, Irish setter, Norwegian elkhound, poodles, schnauzer

Heart Disease (congenital) Collie, poodles, Pomeranian

23

Table 6 *Some Dog Breeds That Have Predispositions Toward Hereditary Physical Disorders (Cont.)*

Kidney Disease	Alaskan malamute, basenji, cocker spaniel, Doberman pinscher, Lhasa apso, Norwegian elkhound, Samoyed, Shih Tzu, standard poodle
Neurological Problems	
Epilepsy	Beagle, German shepherd, poodles, Saint Bernard
Myasthenia gravis (congenital)	Fox terrier, Jack Russell terrier, springer spaniel
Respiratory/Nasal Problems	
Laryngeal paralysis (congenital)	Bouvier des Flandres, sled dogs
Nasal defects (congenital)	Brachycephalic breeds
Soft palate disorders (congenital)	Brachycephalic breeds
Tracheal collapse	Toy breeds
Skeletal Problems	
Jaw disease (craniomandibular osteopathy)	Cairn terrier, Scottish terrier, West Highland white terrier; occasional: boxer, Doberman pinscher, Great Dane, Labrador
Leg joint problems Growth and development defects (shoulder, elbow, knee, ankle)	Large and giant breeds
Hip dysplasia	Large, fast-growing breeds, especially German shepherd, Great Pyrenees, mastiff, retrievers, Saint Bernard
Knee-cap dislocation (patellar luxation—congenital)	Toys; large and giant breeds

Table 6 *Some Dog Breeds That Have Predispositions Toward Hereditary Physical Disorders* (Cont.)

Skin Problems

Cutaneous asthenia (Ehler-Danlos syndrome)	Boxer, springer spaniel
Hair loss	
Color mutant alopecia	Fawn-colored or blue-coated dogs
Ears (pinna alopecia—congenital)	Dachshunds
Growth-hormone responsive dermatosis	Chow chow, keeshond, Pomeranian, poodles
Mast cell tumors	Boston terrier, boxer
Schnauzer comedo syndrome (congenital)	Miniature schnauzer
Zinc-responsive dermatitis	Malamute, Siberian husky

If the breed you have chosen has a known predilection toward a particular genetically transmitted physical disorder, you will want to be particularly careful to satisfy yourself that there is no history of disease in your prospective puppy's background. It is usually recommended that such a search go back at least two generations. Any reliable breeder will be happy to provide this information, and many now include a guarantee in a purchase contract covering a period up to one year should a puppy develop a physical problem. Of course, by then you will have become devoted to your pet, so it's far better to choose wisely in the first place.

BEHAVIOR PROBLEMS BROUGHT ABOUT BY POOR BREEDING AND HANDLING

In addition to physical problems that can occur when puppies are bred with too little attention to or knowledge of genetics, unfortunate behavior characteristics can also be heightened.

Careless handling, too, can either add to poor behavior traits that already exist in a puppy or can actually bring about serious behavior faults. Good, early socialization of a puppy by a breeder is essential if that puppy is to develop into a stable, responsive animal (see *Socialization: The Single Most Important Process in Bringing Up a Happy, Responsive, Satisfactory Puppy*, page 108).

Behavior problems can occur in any breed of dog that has been poorly bred and/or badly socialized. Table 7 lists some dog breeds that are known to have a high propensity toward particular behavior problems when they are improperly bred or socialized. If you are aware of the potential toward a behavior problem in the breed of dog you have chosen, you will be better equipped to judge a puppy intelligently.

SOME CAUTIONS

Unfortunately, popularity often leads to poor breeding. When the demand for a particular breed of dog is greater than the number of puppies available from established breeders, opportunists may step in. These people often have no knowledge of genetics, proper canine health care, or the appropriate socialization steps required for a puppy's emotional stability. The resulting puppies are usually disappointing at best and disastrous at worst.

Be careful not to be taken in by backyard breeders out to make a quick dollar. Do not be lured by advertisements that promise ''show quality'' or ''AKC registered'' puppies at bargain prices. Remember, when it

Table 7 *Behavior Problems Toward Which the Following Breeds Have a Propensity when Poorly Bred and Badly Socialized [Note: These Problems Can Occur in Any Poorly Bred and Socialized Breed]*

Breed	Antisocial	Overaggressive	Destructive	Hard to Train	High-strung, Excitable, Restless	Irritable, Snappish	Overstubborn	Overterritorial, Guarding	Timid, Nervous, Neurotic	Unstable	Yappy
Alaskan malamute	X	X	X					X			
American cocker spaniel	X	X				X				X	X
Beagle				X		X	X	X			
Belgians			X	X	X		X	X	X		
Borzoi		X									
Boston terrier	X					X			X		
Boxer		X		X	X				X		
Brittany spaniel			X		X			X			
Collie					X	X			X	X	
Dachshund						X				X	

Table 7 *Behavior Problems Toward Which the Following Breeds Have a Propensity when Poorly Bred and Badly Socialized [Note: These Problems Can Occur in Any Poorly Bred and Socialized Breed]* (Cont.)

Breed	Antisocial	Overaggressive	Destructive	Hard to Train	High-strung, Excitable, Restless	Irritable, Snappish	Overstubborn	Overterritorial, Guarding	Timid, Nervous, Neurotic	Unstable	Yappy
Doberman pinscher		X			X						
German shepherd		X						X		X	
Great Pyrenees					X				X		
Greyhound					X					X	
Irish setter										X	
Minature schnauzer						X		X		X	
Old English sheepdog			X	X	X	X	X	X	X		
Poodle (especially toys)		X			X	X		X		X	X
Saint Bernard	X						X		X	X	
Shetland sheepdog					X			X			X

28

Table 7 *Behavior Problems Toward Which the Following Breeds Have a Propensity when Poorly Bred and Badly Socialized [Note: These Problems Can Occur in Any Poorly Bred and Socialized Breed]* (Cont.)

Breed	Antisocial	Overaggressive	Destructive	Hard to Train	High-strung, Excitable, Restless	Irritable, Snappish	Overstubborn	Overterritorial, Guarding	Timid, Nervous, Neurotic	Unstable	Yappy
Weimaraner			X	X	X		X				
West Highland white terrier					X	X	X				
Yorkshire terrier								X			X

29

comes to well-bred, carefully raised puppies, you get what you pay for. That doesn't necessarily mean you have to pay a king's ransom for a good pet dog. Many good, responsible breeders will part with what they call a "pet quality" puppy that doesn't quite live up to exacting show standards for an excellent price. But you do not want to sacrifice good genetics and responsible care—attention to physical and emotional health—to save a few dollars.

By the same token, watch out for puppy stores. In these establishments you are apt to pay top dollar for a puppy about which you know absolutely nothing except what a store employee is willing or able to tell you. Puppies sold to retail stores are often raised in very poor conditions; they have usually been taken away from the litter too early in order to preserve their "cuteness" for the longest possible period of time and have traveled for days under adverse conditions. Because of this and the too-early proximity to strange animals, a puppy may be harboring an illness that will probably not surface until after the "forty-eight-hour (or whatever) guarantee" has long since expired (see *Preventive Medicine: Immunizations,* page 56). What is more, the potential for both physical and behavior problems due to poor breeding, poor or nonexistent socialization, and trauma are legion.

FINDING THE BEST

How do you find the best? There are several sources for healthy puppies available to you if you take a little time and effort. If someone you know owns a good example of the breed of dog you're interested in, find out where that person got his dog. Ask one or more local veterinarians for advice about breeders in your area. Talk to breeders at a dog show. Contact the American Kennel Club (AKC)* for a list of recognized breeders in your

* American Kennel Club, 51 Madison Avenue, New York, NY 10010.

geographic vicinity. Check your local library for breed publications; these often have lists of breed clubs and organizations.

Once you have found one or more breeders who specialize in the type of dog you want, you will want to visit the kennel if it is close enough, meet the dam (and sire, if possible), see the puppies if they have already been born, and check the litter's background to assure yourself as far as possible that the particular ''line'' of dogs does not have hereditary physical or behavioral problems. (See Tables 8 and 9 in the following chapter for health and behavior guidelines.)

All little puppies are cute and appealing, a fact that unscrupulous and careless breeders and sellers count on. But don't forget that you will be investing a great deal more than money in your puppy's upbringing—love and care and time—so don't be satisfied with less than the best to begin with.

Choosing a Veterinarian

If your puppy's breeder is local, you may want to continue to use whatever veterinarian has been taking care of your puppy since before birth. If not, the breeder may be able to recommend a veterinarian in your area. Responsible dog-owning friends can also help. Failing any of these, the American Animal Hospital Association (AAHA), an organization devoted to maintaining high standards in veterinary hospitals, can provide you with a list of member hospitals in your area.*

It is a good idea to visit one or more veterinarians

---

* American Animal Hospital Association (AAHA), P.O. Box 15899, Denver, CO 80215-0899.

before you get your puppy. Choosing a veterinarian is a lot like choosing a doctor for yourself and your family. No matter how well recommended a veterinarian is, how many excellent professional organizations he or she belongs to, and how much modern equipment is in the office, if you aren't comfortable with the doctor yourself, you won't be happy.

Depending on where you live, you may be able to choose between an elaborate hospital with a staff of dozens, a group practice consisting of three or four veterinarians, or a doctor who practices alone. With all of the advances that are continuously being made in veterinary medicine, it is important to know that the doctor you choose has access to specialists and equipment that your dog might require in the future.

Ask questions, look around, and satisfy yourself that the hospital or clinic is clean and well equipped. Find out about fees, methods of payment, office hours, telephone times, what provisions are made for off-hour emergencies, and any other details you may want to know.

Once you have chosen a veterinarian, make an appointment right away to take your new puppy in for a complete physical examination as soon as you get it.

Space Management

Before you bring your new puppy home, you and your family will have to make some important decisions about space management. This is an important factor in raising a puppy successfully. Intelligent space management protects a puppy from harm and saves your home from damage. It also helps you teach your puppy acceptable behavior in a number of areas with minimum hassle.

As the primary living space for a puppy we recommend that you choose a room such as the kitchen, a large bathroom, or the basement (depending on the size of the puppy and the layout of your house or apartment). Try to choose a room that is not isolated from family activity. Confine the puppy with a gate (baby-gate, dog-gate, for example) rather than closing the door so that the puppy does not feel cut off from household activities and can see, hear, and smell what is going on and who is coming and going. This, by the way, is also ideal if you already have an adult animal in the house; the two animals can become acquainted gradually through the gate.

This room will be the primary living area of your puppy until it is entirely housebroken, and the floor should be covered with newspaper (see *Errorless Housebreaking*, page 119). It should also be puppy-proofed. Look at the entire area from a puppy's-eye view and remove anything that might be dangerous to your puppy when it is left alone: dangling electric wires, small chewable or swallowable objects, containers of chemicals, and cleaning solutions or paints. Remember that as your puppy grows it will be able to jump up on furniture and stand on its hind legs to reach things.

If you decide that the puppy will be allowed to sleep in a bedroom with a family member, see *The First Night*, page 50.

We are set firmly against the use of crates or cages for puppy space management in the home, despite their advocacy by a number of dog-care "experts." There are several reasons for this: Their use is often abused by owners who find it so easy and convenient to close a dog in a crate that they continue to do so long after the dog is grown. Most crates are too small and too uncomfortable for all but the smallest and most inactive dogs. What is more, they deprive a puppy of the opportunity to explore its surroundings on a continuing basis. A puppy should be free to experience a variety of sensations at will, including being able to get up, stretch out, sit down, and walk around whenever it feels like it. Even more important, a crate (or even a bed) of its "own" encourages a puppy to become territorial. If your puppy has a strong territorial instinct to begin with (if it is a terrier, for example), you will be abetting this instinct and may succeed in fostering territorial aggression in your pet. By the way, it is simply not true that a puppy will not eliminate in a crate because it is its bed, an argument often put forth by advocates of crates for dogs. It will if it has to.

There are only two times when a crate or cage should be used for a puppy. The first is during travel. Obviously, a puppy must be confined in some manner if it is going to travel in a public conveyance. A small- or middle-sized puppy can be transported in a carrying case, but a large puppy will need a crate. Some owners and breeders advocate the use of a carrier or crate for all car travel, for the dog's safety. The other time when a large crate or a baby's playpen is useful is if a puppy or dog is recovering from surgery or a serious illness and must be kept quiet. A crate can then be put in the middle of the living room, kitchen, or family room so that the puppy can be near people while remaining safely off its feet.

Equipment Needed

Don't be lured by advertisements in catalogues and immense displays of goods in pet-supply stores to purchase more than you need for your puppy. Later on you may want to add a toy or two, a fancy collar, or other luxury items, but for now you don't need much, so keep your purchases simple.

Your most important piece of equipment is a sturdy, good-quality tension or folding gate of some sort. These can usually be found in baby furniture stores, pet stores, or hardware stores. Choose a gate that can be easily opened or put up and down for human access, but that will not collapse readily when an ever-stronger puppy jumps up on it. If you are getting a small-breed puppy, be sure that any openings between slats or at the edges are not big enough for the puppy to get its head through. A puppy's head may be a lot smaller than a baby's, and you may have to tack a covering of coated wire or screening on the inside of the gate to prevent an accident.

As we said above, we are firmly against commercial-type dog beds as well as crates. You do not want to foster territorial behavior in a puppy by letting it believe that a particular place belongs to it. One of the most satisfactory "beds" for a puppy is a piece of fake fur. It is washable, soft, and cuddly, and for some reason most puppies do not chew on it. But most important, it is portable. A piece of fake fur can be picked up at a five-and-ten or remnant store and will soon become a wonderful "security blanket" for your puppy. It can go along to the veterinarian, the boarding kennel, and on car trips—wherever the puppy goes. In the absence of some fake fur, an old sweater or blanket will do, but it will not be as indestructible or as washable and is apt to be chewed.

You will probably want to purchase a couple of large, heavy (untippable) ceramic bowls—one for water and the other for food—although any old heavy china dishes will do. High-impact plastic is all right for most dogs, although some animals do develop contact skin allergies to plastic. Soft, molded plastic will not do for puppies because it is too easily chewed into pieces that can be swallowed. Metal bowls are often too light and can be tipped and loudly tossed around, and they often pit when water is kept in them. Whatever type of bowls you choose, they should withstand washing in hot, sudsy water without damage.

Rawhide chew-bones should be part of your pre-puppy purchases. You want to have them handy in order to stop your puppy from nipping you right away (see *Inappro-priate Chewing, Mouthing, Biting, and Pica*, page 140), and be sure to note the warning about safe chew toys on page 141.

Unless you have access to your puppy before you bring it home, you may have to wait to measure its neck before you purchase a collar and leash, equipment you should get right away. (See *Accustom Your Puppy to Wearing a Collar and Leash*, page 151).

Wait until you pick up your puppy or can talk to the breeder before you lay in a supply of food because you should continue feeding it whatever brand and form of food it has been accustomed to.

And remember: Don't recycle your newspapers for a few weeks. You need an ample supply!

Who Will Do What?

Little puppies' needs are not very complicated, but they must be attended to reliably. Before you bring your puppy home you should give some thought to how you and your family will meet these needs; otherwise, the puppy may get lost in the shuffle while everyone argues about who is supposed to do what and when.

Some tasks, such as feeding and entertaining a puppy, are more fun than others—cleaning up soiled papers, for instance—so an equitable division of chores has to be worked out. As we mentioned in Chapter I, before a puppy is a reality in a household young children are apt to make wild promises that they cannot possibly fulfill about how they will do "everything" for their new pet. Adults must be realistic about what to expect from children, and they should also realize that once the novelty of puppy ownership wears off a bit, children will proba-bly have to be reminded to perform even the simplest of care tasks. But even very young children can and should participate. For instance, they can be "helpers" in almost every task.

Another all-too-frequent trap that families sometimes fall into is the "It's *your* dog, you take care of it" syndrome. This is particularly apt to occur when an unpleasant or time-consuming job comes up unexpectedly—a walk in the sleet or rain, a bath to remove mud or tar, handpicking burrs from a coat, a cleanup after diarrhea or vomiting, and so forth. It can turn into a really sticky situation, especially if everyone is rushed or tired (as is usually the case in these instances). The puppy often ends up suffering when this happens—either being made to feel somehow guilty or being handled roughly or carelessly. It is asking a lot for the average family to do, but if you can try to anticipate such situations, perhaps you can come to some advance idea of how to handle them. One way to avoid some of the pressure and bad feelings that can occur when unanticipated accidents and cleanups crop up is to agree ahead of time that the puppy belongs to *all* family members and is everybody's responsibility.

The major puppy-care tasks to consider when you decide who will do what are feeding, cleaning up the environment, cleaning/grooming the puppy itself, exercise and play, trips to the veterinarian (keeping track of immunizations and so on), and training or teaching the puppy how to behave.

Some families get along best with a written schedule. Certainly, if young children are involved, a chart or schedule that can be followed easily and marked off works best. It not only reminds a child when to do what but gives him the satisfaction of being able to check off his task when it is accomplished. A lot depends, of course, on how many people are in a family, what their ages and abilities are, and what each person's own schedule is, but some kind of rotating job chart can be made up for a month at a time and posted in a prominent place with a handy pencil attached on a string for checking off each job as it is done. It may be easiest for some families if one person is responsible for each morning's care, another the afternoon, and so forth; or it may be best for one person to be in charge of feeding each meal for a week or three days, and another for exercising for that same period. Whatever you work out, remember that the novelty wears off in time, especially for children, and that perhaps more variety has to be worked into the schedule as time goes by. As the puppy grows and family members' schedules change during the year, you may find that you have to work out an entirely new system. The important thing is that puppy is cared for and that everyone in the family feels he or she is an equal participant in that care according to his or her ability. Table 8, a Sample Puppy Care Chart for a family of four with two school-age children and two adults who work outside the home, is on the following page.

One final word needs to be added about family participation in puppy-rearing: Although each family member should have input in discussions about the basics of a puppy's behavior parameters, one adult should have the ultimate say in what a puppy is allowed to do and what is it not. Decide ahead of time which parent should make the final decisions (based on a democratic vote, if possible) as to whether or not a puppy is allowed to sleep in a bedroom, get up on the furniture, stay in the dining room during meals, and so forth. These decisions should then be adhered to by everyone. Otherwise, the puppy receives contradictory messages from various family members, and confusion will reign!

Planning Ahead

Table 8 *Sample Puppy Care Chart*

MONTH: _____

Next veterinary appointment: _____	First Week	Second Week	Third Week	Fourth Week
Morning				
Feeding: Wash food and water bowls; give fresh food/water	Joey	Sue	Mother	Dad
Cleanup: Pick up all soiled papers; put down fresh paper	Sue	Joey	Dad	Mother
Exercise/play: Spend at least a half hour play- ing, walking	Dad	Mother	Sue	Joey
Security: Check to be sure there is nothing potentially harmful in the room; be sure gate is firmly in place	Mother	Dad	Joey	Sue
Afternoon				
Feeding	Joey	Sue	Joey	Sue
Cleanup	Sue	Joey	Sue	Joey
Play/exercise/training	Joey	Sue	Joey	Sue
Evening				
Play/exercise/training	Mother	Dad	Sue	Joey
Grooming	Joey	Sue	Mother	Dad
Bedtime				
Exercise	Dad	Mother	Dad	Mother
Feeding	Mother	Dad	Mother	Dad
Security	Dad	Mother	Dad	Mother

3

The Big Day

The big day has arrived. You are about to go and pick up your puppy from the breeder to bring it home. You probably made a specific appointment ahead of time; otherwise, it's a good idea to call the breeder before you leave home. She knows when it is best for the puppy to travel—usually not too soon after a meal.

If you have already purchased a piece of fake fur for your puppy, bring it along. It is also a good idea to bring a cardboard carton lined with newspaper for the puppy to sit in or lie in in the car. Nerves and excitement will probably cause the puppy to urinate, or it may have an attack of diarrhea or car sickness—all of which are easier to cope with in a paper-lined carton than on someone's lap or the car's seat. If you are bringing the puppy home via public transportation, however, you will need a sturdy paper-lined carrying case.

Choosing a Puppy

If you have been able to visit the breeder ahead of time and have met the puppies, you may already have made your choice. Puppies do change a lot very quickly, though, and you may want to reconsider when you arrive at the breeder's, if you have that option.

JUDGING HEALTH

If you have not met the puppies before or have not made a firm decision as to which puppy you want, there are several things you shoulder consider when making your choice. Do not take a puppy that does not appear to be in excellent health with the mistaken notion that it has only a "slight cold" or some such. You are asking for serious trouble, and it is highly possible that your puppy will not live to grow up.

It is not a good idea to select the smallest puppy in the litter (the "runt") for several reasons. Sometimes the runt has a congenital physical problem, such as a heart or kidney condition or some other birth defect, that may not be immediately evident but that has prevented it from utilizing its food properly in order to grow. Even if there is no underlying physical problem, the fact that a puppy has not grown as much as its littermates probably indicates it has not received enough nourishment. Whatever the reason, the runt usually grows up to be a delicate, sickly dog that requires more than normal medical care and owner attention.

Table 9 is a general checklist for selecting a healthy puppy. If you are new at puppy ownership, it is a good idea to take the list with you when you go to select your puppy. It is easy to overlook potential problems when you are looking at several adorable puppies. Add to this the confusion of several family members trying to decide

41

Table 9 *Physical Checklist for Selecting a Healthy Puppy
(Take this list with you when you go to select a puppy.)*

	Good Sign	Possible Problem
Pen, yard, enclosure	Clean, no offensive odors	Excrement, foul or strong disinfectant odors
Puppy's		
Eyes	Clear, clean	Cloudy eyes, matter in corners, watering, squinting in light
Ears	Clean, no odor	Matter in ears, bad odor, ear flap dirty or caked, sensitive to touch, scratching ears
Mouth	Clean, no bad odor, gums pink and firm	Bad odor, bleeding gums, coated tongue, drooling, sensitive, discoloration
Nose	Dry or slightly damp, cool	Discharge, caked matter around, hot
Abdomen	Firm but not hard, slightly rounded	Distended, hard to the touch, or flabby and wrinkled, sensitive
Rectum	Clean, pink	Dried fecal matter, red and sore-looking
Genitals	Clean, pink; males—2 testes	Red and sore-looking, pus, undescended testicle(s)
Foot pads	Firm, clean	Sore, cut or torn, nails ragged
Coat	Clean, shiny	Ragged-looking, dirty, bare spots

Table 9 *Physical Checklist for Selecting a Healthy Puppy*
(Take this list with you when you go to select a puppy.)
(Cont.)

	Good Sign	Possible Problem
Skin	Pink, clean, odorless, firm and elastic but not tight	Lumps, bumps, red spots, bad or disinfected odor, lack of elasticity, dry, flaky
Rib cage	Firm, barrel-like, can feel ribs	Frail-feeling, sore to the touch
Spine	Straight, even	Bumps, knobs, sore to the touch
Overall appearance	Looks healthy and happy	Looks sickly

which puppy is cutest, and the possible influence of the breeder, you may be pressured into making a hasty decision.

Don't let this happen. Take your time and look over each puppy individually. You should pick up the puppy and give it a thorough eye and hand check.

Eyes, ears, mouth, nose, and rectal area should be clean, pink but not red, and have no discharge at all or any bad odor. Any sign of diarrhea, a cough, or runny nose or eyes can be an indication of canine distemper or another infectious disease; or the puppy could have a serious worm infestation. Bad-smelling ears or matter in the canals can be due to an infection and, if a puppy's ear flap appears red or itchy, the puppy probably has ear mites. Bad breath or a coated tongue can be general signs of ill health, and bleeding or discolored gums may signify anemia or a bleeding disorder.

Look at the puppy's feet and foot pads. Sore-looking feet or torn nails can be signs that the puppy has been kept in a cage with rough wire flooring or in some other uncomfortable area. A puppy with sore feet has obviously not been cared for well.

Feel the puppy's body. Run both hands over the entire length of the puppy from head to tail. Pay particular attention to the spine and rib cage. There should be no bumps or protrusions, and the skeleton should feel firm, the spine straight and even. Run your palm over the puppy's stomach. It should be rounded and firm. If it feels bloated or hard, the puppy may be suffering from some digestive problem or may be badly infested with roundworms. The genitals should be pink and tiny. Undescended testicles are very common in male puppies and can be a hereditary trait. Sometimes they descend later on, but they usually are descended at birth. If you cannot feel both testes in a puppy you may not want to take a chance that they will appear as the puppy gets older. Testicular cancer is very common in older dogs with undescended testicles.

Put the puppy down on the ground and encourage it to walk a bit. All young puppies waddle and weave some, especially if they are heavy, but you want to be sure the puppy does not limp or act as if its legs or feet are weak or hurting.

Last but by no means least, look at the puppy's coat and skin. The coat should be smooth and shiny with no bare patches; the skin should be smooth, odorless, and pink or white. Skin and haircoat problems are legion and extremely difficult to diagnose and treat; they can range from bacterial infections to mange to parasitic infestations and many others. You do *not* want to take on a puppy with a dermatologic problem!

Once you have satisfied yourself that the puppy of your choice is in good health, take the time to check out its behavior.

JUDGING BEHAVIOR

In Chapter 6 and throughout this book we talk a great deal about socialization and its importance in raising a behaviorally sound dog. There is usually no way that you can judge exactly how well a breeder has socialized a puppy unless you can observe the puppy's daily life with the breeder. It is a good sign if you know satisfactory puppies or dogs that have been raised in the same kennel. A few simple tests that you can perform will tell you something about how the puppy reacts to people and to its environment. Table 10 will help you do this.

We mentioned some of the physical reasons why you do not want to select the runt of the litter. There are behavioral reasons as well. A runt may be tiny because it is extremely timid and has not been able to stand up to its littermates to get the proper nutrition; or it may be a genetically withdrawn animal and be malnourished because it isn't in its nature to stand up for its rights. Whichever the reason, the puppy will be very difficult for an inexperienced owner to handle.

An extremely assertive puppy can be very difficult to handle, too. It can become overly aggressive, especially if the breed you have chosen is naturally aggressive. Unless you are willing and able to seize and retain a dominant role over that puppy, you will have problems. While we're on the topic of aggression, be sure to heed the warning that we give in *Nip Aggression in the Bud* (page 146) and do not get a puppy before it is at least seven weeks old (preferably eight). If you do, you will have to teach it the limits of aggressive behavior yourself instead of letting its littermates do the job.

Therefore, you do not want to choose either the feistiest or the quietest puppy in the litter but one that is somewhere in between the two. You usually can identify the puppies' roles by observing the litter at play for a few minutes.

The other "tests" in Table 10 are self-explanatory. They are designed to ascertain that a puppy has been exposed regularly to people and normal household noises by the breeder. If it has not, you would be taking an enormous chance that the puppy will develop serious behavior problems. At the very least you may have to work constantly with your puppy throughout its life to make up for lost time.

Questions to Ask the Breeder

Once you have made your selection, discuss the puppy's care with the breeder. Some breeders have very definite, specific advice to give about every aspect of a puppy's care while others do not. Many give new owners elaborate lists or pages of instructions. Although you will want to pay attention to what the breeder thinks is best, of course, you may not want to slavishly follow all the instructions. If, say, a breeder strongly recommends the use of a cage or crate (and many do), we hope you will decide you do not want to follow that advice (see *Space Management*, page 32). Don't argue, however, or you may find that you are up against a very strong-willed person; it is not unheard of for a breeder to decide that someone is not a suitable adopter.

Find out what immunizations the puppy has been given; if possible, get a written record to give to the veterinarian. You may want to ask the breeder to recommend a veterinarian if you have not already selected one. If a puppy has had any surgery—tail docking or ear clipping, for instance—be sure to obtain detailed care instructions.

It is very important to continue feeding a puppy whatever it has become used to eating, at least at first. You can

Table 10 *Behavioral Checklist for Selecting a Puppy*
(Take this list with you when you go to select a puppy.)

	Good sign	**Possible Problem**
Socialization to Environment		
Clap your hands, slam a door, or make a loud noise	Perks up ears, tilts head, looks at you, possibly stands or sits up, may bark	Jumps, put ears down, tail between legs, lies flat, growls, trembles
Play music, on a radio or tape machine	Perks up ears, looks interested	Same as above
Pick puppy up and put it down on ground outside pen or enclosure	Sits quietly, sniffs ground, gets up and walks around with head and tail up, perks ears	Sits or lies flat with ears and head down, trembles, acts frightened
Socialization to Humans		
Lean or squat on puppy's level, offer hand, palm up	Sniffs hand, acts interested, possibly licks	Backs away acts frightened, growls, barks, may nip
Stroke gently on top of head and along back	Wags tail, possibly licks hand, may roll over	Backs off growls, tries to nip hand or acts frightened, trembles
Pick up, holding firmly but not tightly	Tries to lick your face, may squirm but acts unafraid	Cringes, frightened, struggles wildly, may nip, growl
With puppy on ground, walk past quickly	Sits quietly and gets up and begins to follow you	Cringes, lies flat, growls, may nip at your ankles

Table 10 *Behavioral Checklist for Selecting a Puppy
(Take this list with you when you go to select a puppy.)*
(Cont.)

	Good sign	Possible Problem
Interaction with littermates		
	Plays, licks, may wrestle and growl; acts interested and friendly, holds its own but isn't a bully	Sits very quietly, doesn't enter in; timid, always gets the worst *or* growls, attacks others aggressively, bites, sometimes savagely

change its diet later on if you wish (see *Feeding*, page 64), but you do not want to upset its digestive system now with an abrupt change of diet. If possible, have the breeder give you several days' supply of food in case it is difficult to obtain for some reason. Many breeders do this automatically.

Ask if the breed you have chosen has special coat-care requirements or any other particular physical care idiosyncrasies that you may not be aware of. Sometimes a breeder gives or offers to sell you a booklet about the breed. These booklets can be very helpful, especially if you are not familiar with the breed and its characteristics.

Bringing the Puppy Home: A Stop at the Veterinarian's

If you are going home in a car, put the puppy in the carton you have brought and put the carton on the seat or floor of the car. If you're alone, it is best to put the carton on the floor of the back seat so that if the puppy gets out it won't manage to get under your feet while you drive.

Try to bring someone else with you to keep an eye on the puppy and reassure it.

As we mentioned above, the puppy may eliminate or get car sick on the way home. If there are children in the car, tell them not to shriek or make a fuss if this happens and not to pick up the puppy. Grabbing it around the stomach will only make matters worse. Stroke the puppy's head and speak to it softly. Very often the motion of the car puts the puppy to sleep.

If you are traveling on public transportation, put the carrying case on the floor, if possible, to avoid soiling a seat, and try to reassure the puppy verbally. Again, the motion may put it to sleep in a short time.

If you have other pets at home, it is particularly important to stop at the veterinarian's office on your way home with your puppy. Many puppy diseases are highly contagious to other dogs, and both intestinal and external parasites are easily passed along to both cats and dogs. You do not want to take a chance of introducing germs or parasites into your home. This is especially true if you have an older pet. Even if you do not have other pets, the puppy should be checked over to be sure that it is all right and has no serious congenital problems. This should be done before you have a chance to become attached to it and is especially advisable if you decided not to follow our advice and have obtained your puppy from a pet store or unreliable breeder. Although some disorders may not show up immediately, there are many problems that can be detected in a thorough physical examination, and it is far better to find out about them right away.

If you cannot stop at the veterinarian's on the way home, you should keep the puppy isolated from any other pets until it has had a thorough checkup.

Settling In

No matter how outgoing and friendly it may be, a puppy that has been taken away from its mother and littermates and is surrounded by unfamiliar people and objects is bound to feel lonely and strange at first. The most important thing you and your family can do is help it to feel secure in its new environment. You can accomplish this best by being calm and reassuring and protecting it from too much noise, confusion, or handling.

Do not allow children to overwhelm the puppy even though it is kindly meant. Put the puppy in the space you have already prepared for it with its fake fur or other blanket and a bowl of water, and leave it alone for a while to explore or go to sleep. Do not feed it immediately; because of the excitement of the trip home and the new environment, it may not be hungry or may throw up if it does eat. After a while, one or two people can go in and pet it, but don't allow a lot of people in the room at once or the puppy may become frightened. Let it become accustomed gradually to family members and other pets.

Do not attempt to train it, teach it, or discipline it at all until it seems secure in its new environment. Usually, this takes only one or two days.

Follow whatever feeding schedule it has been used to. If the puppy is very nervous or upset and does not eat, one adult can try to coax it quietly until it regains its appetite, but do not make a habit of this or soon the puppy won't eat unless that person is present.

THE FIRST NIGHT

If you have only one puppy, the first night may be difficult. An older pet that you already have may provide some comfort for the puppy just by its very presence in the house, even if it is not yet allowed in the same room.

Your instinct will be to comfort your puppy when it becomes lonely and cries or whimpers, as it most certainly will. The problem is that if you give in to this instinct, you immediately teach the puppy its first lesson—that it can get you to do what it wants by crying or whining. Don't be fooled into thinking that your puppy won't figure this out because it's so young—it will. Soon your puppy will have you trained to respond to its every whim.

Start right from the beginning. Decide where you want your puppy to sleep for the rest of its life. You cannot start a puppy off in your bedroom, say, then decide that it has grown too much or snores too much and should accept the kitchen as its new bedroom. That is harder on it than one or two lonely nights in the beginning.

Wherever it sleeps must be a large enough area of confinement for plenty of newspaper because a small puppy urinates and defecates several times during the night. *If* you have decided ahead of time that the puppy will be allowed to sleep in a bedroom, you have to cordon off part of the room. If the puppy is small, a child's playpen will do, or you can close off an alcove, a large walk-in closet or dressing room, or an adjoining bathroom. Be sure that wherever you choose is warm enough for the puppy.

Feed the puppy just before bedtime so that it is full and comfortable. Put it in the area you have chosen with its fake fur. The old trick of a ticking clock still works for some puppies. Wrap a wind-up clock with a loud tick in several layers of toweling and place it next to the puppy's "bed." The sound of the ticking is reminiscent of the sound of the puppy's mother's and siblings' beating hearts and may reassure it.

Wherever the puppy is, it may whine and may even bark. Steel yourself *not* to go and pat it or even speak to it. If you want to be allowed to sleep through the night in the future, you have to ignore the puppy's protestations. Usually the puppy settles down and goes to sleep in a short while. It may wake once or twice during the first night and protest, but again you must ignore it if you don't want to start a bad habit.

You may be surprised at how quickly your puppy learns to stay quiet and sleep by itself at night. Usually it will sleep through the night in just a few days.

4

General Physical Care of a Growing Puppy

You probably have received some instructions from your puppy's breeder about various aspects of your new pet's feeding and general care. This chapter will serve to give you some background details in important areas of puppy care. Your own veterinarian, however, is the best source of information about specifics of your puppy's physical well-being. By observing your puppy, your pet's doctor knows just what is best for it at any given time. Your veterinarian is also aware of particular problems in your geographical area—the outbreak of a contagious disease or the sudden influx of a parasite, for example—and is abreast of new developments in the rapidly changing science of canine veterinary medicine. Always consult your veterinarian if you have questions about any aspect of your puppy's physical care, no matter how seemingly minor.

Illness

Young puppies can become ill very suddenly, and because of their small size, any illness can become serious within a short period of time. Don't wait for any unusual changes in your puppy's normal habits or unexplained symptoms to clear up by themselves. Always call the veterinarian right away.

Never attempt to treat your puppy with home remedies or over-the-counter medications, except with a veterinarian's advice. Many household drugs that are made for human consumption are toxic for dogs (and especially puppies); others are much too strong for a puppy.

It is also a good idea not to use strong household disinfectants and cleansers in your puppy's room or on its food and water dishes. Many puppies have severe allergic reactions to some household products; they may develop skin lesions, breathing difficulty, or intestinal upsets if exposed to these products over an extended period of time.

Accidents

Accidents can occur to puppies even in the best-run households. In general, if your puppy has an accident, it is best not to attempt to give first aid. You may only make matters worse and waste time getting the puppy to the veterinarian.

If your puppy has fallen from a height or been hit by a moving vehicle, always have it checked out immediately even if there are no outward signs of injury. In case of any trauma, you must assume that the puppy is in shock. Keep it warm and quiet, move it as little as possible. Place it in a box or carton, or wrap it snugly in a blanket, and take it to the veterinarian.

Electrocution caused by chewing on a plugged-in electric cord is a very common puppy accident. If you come home and find your puppy unconscious or having trouble breathing, suspect electrical shock and get immediate veterinary help. Don't waste time looking for the cord the puppy may have chewed. But if you find the puppy with its mouth still on a cord, be sure to unplug the cord before touching the puppy.

There are some exceptions to the rule above about not giving first aid to a puppy. If your puppy is bleeding severely, you must try to slow or stop the bleeding before you transport it to the veterinarian or it could bleed to death very quickly. A soft compression, or pressure, bandage is most effective, applied wherever the bleeding is. Several layers of clean material should be pressed directly over the wound and held firmly in place by hand. If there is no one else around to hold the bandage in place while you take the puppy to the doctor, you can tie it in place with a soft strip of cloth. Do *not* tie anything tight enough to constrict blood flow, however. This can be very dangerous.

Another instance in which first-aid measures should be used is if a puppy is suffering from an attack of hypoglycemia, or low blood sugar. This usually occurs only with small-breed puppies when they haven't eaten enough for some reason. It is manifested by weakness, confusion, an inability to stand up, and eventual collapse. If you notice that your small puppy has these symptoms, you should immediately give it some honey, corn syrup, sugar-water, or anything containing sugar. Spoon the mixture directly into the puppy's mouth, a little at a time, until it has swallowed about a tablespoonful. Then take it directly to the veterinarian to ascertain the cause of the problem.

If you know that your puppy has swallowed something poisonous that is noncorrosive—human medicine, antifreeze, or rat poison, for example—you should try to make it vomit as quickly as possible, before the poison can be absorbed in its body. Give it enough hydrogen peroxide by mouth to make it throw up. Don't worry about giving too much hydrogen peroxide—it can't hurt the puppy, but will just make it throw up more. Do *not* give it to the puppy if you are in any doubt as to what it has ingested or if you know that it has swallowed something corrosive, such as gasoline, oil, or anything with lye in it. In a case of lye swallowing, milk can be given to help prevent burning of the esophagus and stomach, but don't waste time with this if it will delay immediate veterinary treatment. A puppy that has swallowed anything potentially poisonous (and this includes all kinds of human medicines, drugs, tobacco, and so forth) should always be seen immediately by a veterinarian because it probably requires further treatment in order to prevent permanent damage. If you cannot reach a veterinarian right away, call your nearest poison control center for instructions.

Preventive Medicine: Immunizations

Periodic physical examinations are an important aspect of good preventive medicine for a growing puppy. When he sees your puppy at regular intervals, your veterinarian can assess the puppy's overall health, weight gain, and growth, and can often spot any sign of difficulty before it becomes a serious problem. When a puppy is growing up, regular physical checkups usually coincide with an immunization schedule.

All growing puppies need a series of immunizations, or "shots," to protect them from infectious diseases. A vaccination causes a puppy's body to form antibodies, or active immunity, against disease.

Although a puppy will have received passive immunity during the first few days of life from its mother's first milk (colostrum), there is currently no widely available way to tell exactly how long these maternal antibodies against disease are present in individual puppies. While they are present, vaccines are automatically inactivated. It is known, however, that they are no longer present in the majority of puppies at about sixteen weeks of age. At this time a vaccination gives a puppy active immunity against disease.

Because of the uncertainty as to when maternal immunity actually wears off, most veterinarians recommend that a puppy receive immunizations at regular intervals, usually every four weeks, so that there is no time when it is unprotected. Although the breeder from whom you get your puppy will usually have begun a vaccination series (often called "temporary" shots), your puppy is not fully protected until it has received the entire series of vaccinations.

It is very important to protect a puppy against possible exposure to infectious disease until the immunization series has been completed. Infectious canine diseases can be transmitted through contact with stools and saliva of infected dogs, by airborne viruses, direct contact with an infected dog, and even via flies and mosquitoes. This is why it is so important not to take your puppy into public places or even into parks and streets frequented by other dogs until your veterinarian has pronounced it fully protected. Some veterinarians recommend keeping a puppy indoors entirely until its vaccination series has been completed. Your veterinarian can best advise you about how to protect your puppy from contagion, based on knowledge of the presence of disease in your area and the degree of protection your puppy has received.

Immunizations can protect puppies (and dogs) against canine distemper, hepatitis, leptospirosis (often combined in one vaccine called DHL), parainfluenza (CPI), canine parvovirus, and rabies.

Heartworm disease is prevented by oral medication in various forms. It is given only after a blood test has determined that there are no heartworms already present in a puppy's bloodstream. Heartworm larvae are transmitted from dog to dog via a mosquito bite, so the period of time that your puppy must be protected against the disease is affected by the weather (and mosquito season) in the area in which you live. Your veterinarian can advise you about when to proceed with the test and medication for your puppy. Usually this test is given for the first time when a puppy is around six months of age.

Most veterinarians keep records of immunizations and send reminders when boosters are due, but it is a good idea to keep your own records too. We have included a suggestion for a record book for your puppy at the end of this chapter.

Intestinal Parasites

Part of every puppy's first veterinary visit should include a stool-sample evaluation. When you call to make your first appointment, ask if you should bring along a stool sample. Some people believe that all puppies are born with roundworms (Ascarids), others simply that they all have a high potential for roundworms. Whichever the case, they are extremely common canine intestinal parasites. They are often not visible to the naked eye and can be detected only by microscopic evaluation. Left unchecked, roundworms can cause severe diarrhea, vomiting, weight loss, weakness, anemia, and even eventual death in a small puppy.

Because stool evaluations are not always completely accurate and roundworms can be so debilitating for a young puppy, many veterinarians advise automatically deworming a puppy at least once, whether or not worm larvae are visible in the microscopic evaluation, just to be on the safe side. If worms are present in a puppy, several dewormings may be needed over a three- to four-week period in order to rid the animal of all worms and larvae.

A strong caution: Do *not* attempt to deworm your puppy yourself with over-the-counter medications. Worm medications are very strong, and you could make your puppy very sick with an improper dose. What is more, most of these drugs are intended to kill only one particular type of worms, and you could end up with a very sick puppy that still has worms.

Grooming

No matter what kind of coat your puppy has, it should get used to being groomed and handled as soon as you get it. We talk about the importance of this in *Socialization: The Single Most Important Process in Bringing Up a Happy, Responsive, Satisfactory Puppy*, page 108. It is in your own best interest to accustom your puppy to handling early in life. Many situations are sure to arise when you will be glad that your pet trusts you enough to allow you to handle or treat any part of its body without undue fuss. A regular grooming session is also an excellent opportunity to look over your puppy from head to foot.

It is particularly important for long-haired puppies to get used to grooming early in life. Proper care is essential for long coats if they are going to be kept snarl- and mat-free. If a long-haired puppy's coat is allowed to develop snarls or mats, it will be a very unpleasant experience for both of you to get it back in shape. Fortunately, long-haired coats are fairly easy to care for when puppies are young, so by accustoming them to grooming early, you will have a head start when their full coats come in at maturity. In Chapter 1, Table 4, there is a general summary of various care requirements for different kinds of dog coats.

Some dog-care books give a great deal of rather complicated instruction about how and where to groom a dog. In our experience, a young puppy can be groomed just about anywhere that is convenient. If you begin when your puppy is young, there is no need to make grooming a chore for either of you. Depending on the size of your puppy and your own degree of limberness, you can brush or comb your puppy while you both sit on the floor, with your puppy in your lap, with your puppy on a table or counter—in other words, wherever you are both comfortable. Your puppy can sit down, stand up, or lie down; if it is lying down, it will probably go to sleep while you groom it. The only requirement is that it learn to stay quietly until you are finished, when you tell it how good it has been and that it is all right to leave.

Most puppies learn to like being groomed and are only too happy to stay quiet while you are grooming them. Many get into place automatically as soon as you get the comb or brush out. Even very young children can participate in gentle daily brushing and combing, although they should not be allowed to poke or inspect a puppy's mouth, ears, or eyes.

A brush is the best grooming tool for short-haired and wire-haired puppies, while a comb is best for long-haired puppies. Before you brush each area, take your hand and turn the hair back to expose the skin, which should be pinkish and free from spots or dry scaly areas. If you suspect any kind of skin problem, be sure to get immediate veterinary advice. Dermatologic problems can be very hard to correct, and the earlier they are diagnosed and treated the better.

Be sure to either brush or comb every part of your pup, and don't let it prevent you from doing a certain area.

Many puppies don't like to have their legs and feet touched or groomed. If your puppy pulls back when you grasp its leg or foot, it may be the restraint that it objects to more than the grooming. Don't fight with the puppy over this but hold its leg very gently. If even this is a problem, try brushing the puppy's legs without holding on to them, and then simply let each foot rest in the palm of your open hand while you brush or comb it. It may help to let the puppy lie on its side while you work on its feet or legs. Some puppies never learn to like having their feet worked on, and you may need to be firm about it. At first, however, do not make any area of your puppy's body into a battle zone, or soon it will be difficult to groom it at all.

Look over your puppy carefully at least once a week. Begin by stroking your puppy with your hand, from head to tail base, then feeling its body all over with both hands. Look at its eyes, into its ears and mouth, under its tail at its rectal area, and at the bottom of its feet. If there is dried matter at the nose corner of a puppy's eyes, remove it with a damp cloth. Smell your puppy's ears; a bad odor can indicate an ear infection. The insides of its ears should be pinkish and clean-looking. If there is a lot of matter or any black specks inside the ears, suspect ear mites (more about these below). Long-haired puppies often get fecal matter stuck in the hair around the anus. If this has happened, use a damp cloth to clean the area.

The insides of your puppy's mouth should be pink and the gums firm. Ask your veterinarian to show you how to clean your puppy's teeth, a procedure that more and more veterinarians now advise to prevent later problems.

Breeds that require professional coat care should visit the groomer for the first time as soon as they are old enough to be completely immunized. A puppy needn't stay long and may only need to be combed or brushed the first time, but it should begin to be accustomed to going to the groomer as young as possible.

External Parasites

If you have obtained your puppy from a responsible breeder, it should be free of external parasites such as ear mites, fleas, and ticks when you adopt it. However, all of these parasites are extremely contagious among animals, and fleas and ticks are easily picked up from the environment. If your puppy is scratching or biting itself excessively in any part of its body, or if you notice any kind of rash, skin redness, or bare spots in its haircoat, suspect some kind of external parasite and have the veterinarian check the puppy right away. Prompt action is necessary in order to clear up any parasites as quickly as possible. Even if your puppy does not show any obvious outward signs of being infested with an external parasite, be sure to check it over on a regular basis while grooming.

FLEAS

Fleas are the most common canine external parasite. They feed on dogs by sucking their blood, and a severe infestation of fleas can sap a puppy of energy and even cause anemia. In addition, fleas often carry tapeworms. A severe infestation of fleas usually causes scratching, but it is possible for a young puppy to have fleas with no noticeable signs.

While grooming your puppy, turn the hair back and look at its skin for small black spots. This is flea "dirt" and is often visible in the thick fur where the spine meets the tail, around the neck, and under the legs in the puppy's "armpits." If you see flea dirt or fleas themselves, consult your veterinarian about what to do. Remember that the puppy's environment must also be rid of fleas or they will recur.

Never use commercial over-the-counter flea repellants on a puppy or its environment. Too much overly strong insecticide can be poisonous for a puppy and does more harm than good. Young puppies should never wear flea or tick collars.

TICKS

Ticks are not apt to be a puppy problem in most areas, since they are usually picked up when a dog wanders in tall grasses and wooded areas. They are becoming more prevalent in many areas, however, and can be disease carriers, so prompt removal is important if you see a tick on your puppy.

A tick adheres to a puppy's skin, often in damp, dark areas such as inside the ear pinna (flap), in the neck area, at the base of the tail, and underneath the legs. An unengorged tick is small, flat, reddish-brown, and beetlelike. A tick that is engorged with blood looks like a tan bean.

If you see a tick on your puppy, remove it with tweezers and touch the spot with disinfectant; some people recommend touching the skin at the spot of entry with alcohol first to make the tick relax its grip. Put the removed tick in alcohol, lighter fluid, or nail polish remover to kill it—they are very hardy. If your puppy has more than one tick or ticks recur regularly, talk to your veterinarian about environmental control and about the advisability of having the puppy dipped in an anti-tick bath.

EAR MITES

An ear mite infestation causes severe itching which may manifest itself in ear scratching, head shaking, head rubbing, and eventually in an ear discharge and reddened pinnae (ear flaps). Left untreated, ear mites can cause serious ear canal infections. Ear mites are impossible to see with the naked eye, but you should suspect them if you see white specks or a reddish-brown discharge in your puppy's ears or if there is any discharge or matter of any kind in them. Your veterinarian can perform a microscopic examination of the matter to confirm diagnosis.

Ear mites are controlled with specific medication in the form of drops. If there are other cats or dogs in your household, they should also be checked for ear mites which are highly contagious.

Feeding

As we said in the previous chapter, you should always continue to feed your puppy whatever it has been accustomed to eating for at least the first two weeks after you adopt it. Sudden change in diet is a primary cause of diarrhea and other intestinal upsets in young puppies.

CHANGING DIET

If you decide to change your puppy's diet for any reason after that, be sure to do it gradually to avoid problems. Mix a bit of the new food with the old diet for one meal. If the puppy's digestive system accepts this with no problems, you can gradually mix in more new food each day. But go slowly and watch your puppy's stools and appetite closely for signs of upset. At some point you may have to "stall" with a mix for a while before you can switch over to the new food completely. If a new food does not agree with your puppy no matter how slowly you add it, start all over again with a different food. Sometimes there is no apparent reason why a given food or food in a particular form does not agree with an individual puppy. Just as each puppy's personality and temperament are different, some puppies have food idiosyncrasies or are allergic to certain ingredients. If this is the case, you have to work with your puppy to find the diet that best suits it.

NUTRITIONAL NEEDS

As a puppy owner you do not need to learn a great deal about proper puppy nutrition as long as you feed your puppy a well-balanced, complete, commercial diet (more about kinds of food in the next section). However, you might find it helpful to know a few general facts about growing puppies' nutritional needs.

Until it is almost half grown, a growing puppy needs two times more calories (food energy) and nutrients per pound of weight than an adult dog of the same breed. It is usually recommended that this amount by cut back to 1.6 times when a puppy has reached 40 percent of its adult weight, and cut again to 1.2 times when it has reached 80 percent of its adult weight.*

The actual amount of food that you feed your puppy depends in part on how large it is. Smaller breeds require more calories per pound than larger breeds, for example. In general, a healthy puppy will regulate its own food intake pretty well and should usually be allowed to eat all that it will in one feeding—that is, in approximately fifteen minutes—at which point the food should be removed. If a puppy still seems to be hungry after eating all of its food, it should be given more. An alternate method is what we call "ad lib" feeding—leaving dry food out all the time for a puppy to snack on at will. This seems to be particularly helpful in preventing gastric dilation/torsion ("Bloat") in large breeds; it keeps them from gulping down too much food too fast at mealtimes. If you wish, you can add canned, moist food to the dry food for one or two meals while still leaving dry food out the rest of the time. This method will only succeed as long as you do not allow the puppy to eat filling, non-nutritious snacks.

* *Nutrient Requirements of Dogs, Revised 1985.* © 1985 by the National Academy of Sciences.

Planning Ahead

You can judge for yourself if your puppy is thriving. It should be chunky and round-looking with a shiny coat and lots of energy. Don't let your puppy get too fat, however. Check from time to time to be sure that you can still see and feel its ribs under a thin layer of fat. A too-rapid weight gain can put a tremendous strain on a puppy's skeleton, especially on the legs of naturally heavy, large puppies. If you have doubts about exact amounts to feed your puppy, check with your veterinarian.

In order for puppies to digest their food properly, their total intake should be divided into several meals a day (unless you are using the "ad lib" method of feeding). In general, they should be fed four times a day until they are thirteen or fourteen weeks old; three times a day up until six months of age; and twice a day from six months of age until they have reached full growth, at which time they may be given one meal a day.

To grow strong, however, puppies need more than just calories. They require most of the same nutritional elements as other animals. The only basic nutrient for which there is no established minimum requirement for dogs is carbohydrates. Although carbohydrates are a valuable source of energy (calories) for puppies, too much fiber in their diet may prevent the absorption of other nutrients. Vitamin C is synthesized in dogs' bodies and is normally not needed in their diets.*

Table 11 shows the results of some nutritional deficiencies in a puppy's diet.

* *Nutrient Requirements of Dogs, Revised 1985,* © 1985 by the National Academy of Sciences.

Table 11 *Results of Some Deficiencies in a Puppy's Diet*

Nutrient	Result of Deficiency
Calories (energy)	Slow growth: lack of growth; susceptibility to bacterial infection and invasion by parasites
Fat (essential fatty acids)	Coarse, dry hair; skin lesions; infection
Protein and amino acids	Anorexia; severe growth retardation or weight loss; muscle wasting; rough, dull coat
Minerals	
Calcium and phosphorus	Convulsions; poor growth; low appetite; rickets
Potassium	Poor growth; restlessness; muscular paralysis; dehydration; damage to internal organs
Sodium and chlorine	Retarded growth; exhaustion; decreased water intake; dry skin; hair loss
Magnesium	Anorexia; poor weight gain; lack of coordination; irritability; convulsions
Iron and copper	Anemia
Zinc	Retarded weight gain; skin lesions
Iodine	Goiter; skin and skeletal deformities; drowsiness; timidity
Vitamins	
Fat-soluble (excess can be toxic—rarely deficient)	
A	Bone and nerve impairment; eye and skin problems; weight loss

Table 11 *Results of Some Deficiencies in a Puppy's Diet*
(Cont.)

Nutrient	Result of Deficiency
D (must be in balance with calcium and phosphorus)	Rickets
E	Muscle weakness; impaired immune response; retinal degeneration
Water-soluble	
B-complex	Anorexia; failure to grow; weight loss; weakness; anemia; susceptibility to infection

Based on: *Nutrient Requirements of Dogs, Revised 1985,* © *1985 by the National Academy of Sciences.*

WATER

Water is essential for all puppies. It carries nutrients throughout a puppy's body and flushes waste from it. A puppy must drink enough water each day in order to maintain the proper balance of fluid lost through urination, respiration, and evaporation. Because of a number of variables, such as the kind of food a puppy is fed, the puppy's activity level, and environmental temperature, it is impossible to determine the exact amount of water a puppy needs each day, but it has been established that a puppy drinks as much as it needs when given free access to water. Therefore, fresh drinking water should always be available for a puppy to drink at will.

It is never advisable to withhold water from a puppy, as is sometimes recommended during housebreaking. It does not cut back on urination but simply makes the puppy excessively thirsty and can lead to overdrinking and regurgitation when water is offered after a long period.

KINDS OF FOOD

Before we discuss the three principal types of puppy food available on the market, it is important to talk about the quality of the food you give your puppy and its role in preventing dietary deficiency. There is some misconception that all pet foods are essentially the same and that only the packages differ. This is not the case. Although a pet food can meet or exceed recommended *amounts* of nutrients, there is currently no standard against which the *quality* and *usability* of these nutrients is measured. It is possible for a pet food to be "100 percent nutritionally complete" and still deprive a puppy of necessary nutrients.

Recent studies by the College of Veterinary Medicine at the University of Georgia evaluated the growth of puppies fed generic (white-label, or supermarket-label) brands of puppy food and the growth of those fed a well-known national commercial brand. All of the foods claimed to be 100 percent nutritionally complete. The results were dramatic: Puppies fed the generic brands gained less weight, grew less, and in some instances developed skin problems of the sort often associated with a zinc deficiency. The less expensive, generic brands did not deliver the balanced nutrition needed for growing puppies and did not consistently use high-quality ingredients. In many cases, nutritional content was uneven from batch to batch of food, attesting to a lack of quality control. It is not worth the saving of a few dollars to risk this kind of uneven nutrition for your puppy. All of the nationally known pet-food manufacturers have high standards of quality control and base the nutritional content of their products on research and feeding trials. In this instance, you do get what you pay for!

Good-quality commercial puppy food, formulated specifically to meet a growing puppy's high nutritional requirements, gives your puppy the best start in life. Although it is possible to meet a puppy's nutritional needs by feeding it quality adult dog food, you either have to give the puppy an enormous amount of food (resulting in voluminous stools) or supplement the adult food with a high-energy meat diet. It is far easier to feed a food that is designed just for puppies.

Puppy food comes in three basic forms: dry, semimoist, and canned. Each is formulated to be nutritionally complete, and each has advantages and disadvantages as a sole diet.

Dry food is the least expensive. It is low in moisture and lower in nutrients per ounce of food than either of the other varieties. If it is fed to a puppy exclusively, therefore, a fairly large quantity of dry food must be given in order to meet the puppy's caloric and nutritional needs, and water must always be available. Dry food is particularly useful for large-breed puppies that must eat large quantities of food to fulfill their energy requirements. It is the only type of food that can be left out for a puppy to snack on at will, and it is very good for a puppy's teeth and gums.

Semimoist food is somewhat more expensive than dry, and many puppies find it more palatable. Although it has a higher moisture content than dry food, it also must always be fed along with fresh water. Some puppies are apparently allergic to the ingredients that are added to semimoist food in order to keep it moist. It is not as nutritionally dense as canned food but is more nutritious per ounce than dry. It needs no refrigeration and can be left out for short periods of time for self-feeding before it dries up.

Canned puppy food is the most expensive per ounce but the most nutritionally dense and the most universally appealing to puppies. Smaller amounts are needed to meet a puppy's nutritional needs than either of the other forms of food, and for this reason it is generally preferred for small-breed puppies that need concentrated nutrition but cannot eat large quantities. It spoils rapidly after it is opened and cannot be left unrefrigerated for more than a short period of time.

In order to gain the benefits of more than one form of food, many puppy owners opt to feed their puppies a combination of two or more types. They may mix dry and canned food, or dry and semimoist, or feed one or two meals of each per day. Proper nutritional balance won't be sacrificed by mixing types of food as long as each is a high-quality complete diet. You may want to experiment and see which kind (or kinds) of food works best for you and your puppy.

Table 12 summarizes the ingredients found in these three types of commercial foods.

SUPPLEMENTS

Vitamin and mineral supplements are very popular and may even be recommended by some breeders. With some exceptions that only a veterinarian can ascertain, they are not necessary when a puppy is fed a well-balanced commercial diet. Oversupplementation can be harmful to a growing puppy. It can lead to an imbalance of nutrients, which must be maintained in the proper ratio to be effective, and may result in toxicity and even skeletal problems, especially in large-breed puppies.

WHEN TO CHANGE TO ADULT DOG FOOD

Puppy food is extremely rich and high in calories. At some stage, when your puppy is about half grown, puppy food will be too rich for it and will probably cause it to vomit or have diarrhea. This can occur anywhere from six months on, depending on your puppy's size and rate of growth. Watch your puppy carefully, and if it vomits after

71

Table 12 *Examples of Percentages of Ingredients in Three Types of Commercial Dog Foods*

	Dry	Semimoist	Canned
Corn products	68.1	—	—
Meat and bone meal	19.0	—	—
Meat and meat by-products	—	32.8	65–80
Poultry and poultry by-products	—	—	10–20
Soybean meal	7.5	—	—
Soybean/bran flakes	—	32.3	—
Soy flour	—	—	10–20
Soluble carbohydrates	—	21.0	—
Animal fat	4.5	1.0	—
Mineral mix	0.8	3.3	0.5
Vitamin mix	0.1	0.3	0.2
Emulsifiers/solvents/other	—	9.3	—

Adapted from: *Nutrient Requirements of Dogs, Revised 1985,* © 1985 by the National Academy of Sciences.

eating (and you are sure that worms are not the cause), it is time to gradually change over to adult food. Following the suggestions that are made in *Changing Diet* earlier in this section, begin to substitute adult dog food in the same form as the puppy food that you have been using.

Exercise and Play

Throughout this book we emphasize the importance of exercise for all puppies. Exercise does not simply keep a puppy in good physical shape, it also keeps it from becoming bored, restless, and "antsy"—all primary causes of misbehavior. A puppy that has had a good run or play session will be content and tired out, and will usually sleep or rest quietly for some time afterward.

Very young puppies expend a great deal of energy every day just growing and running around. Puppies have soft bones, and their joints are not fully formed; also, large, heavy puppies are particularly apt to develop joint and skeletal problems if they are allowed or encouraged to run or jump too vigorously while they are young. It is usually best to wait until a puppy is around six months of age (possibly older for heavy breeds) before beginning a vigorous exercise routine. Remember, too, that a puppy (or any dog) should not be allowed to exercise immediately after eating. Exercise immediately after eating has been cited as a cause of "Bloat" (gastric dilation/torsion complex), a serious and potentially fatal condition that is especially common in large dogs. Children may need to be cautioned not to be too rough with a young puppy or tire it out too much. A good rule of thumb with a young puppy is to let it set its own limits on playtime. When it is tired, stop. Later on, when the puppy is half grown, is time enough to begin a vigorous exercise routine.

Of course, leash walking can be a large part of your daily exercise, which can begin in public places as soon as your puppy is fully immunized. We describe the procedure for accustoming your pet to walking on a leash in Chapters 8 and 11. Every puppy, no matter how tiny, should be walked on a leash at least twice a day—more often, if possible. No matter how large your yard or enclosure may be, your puppy will become very bored with it if that is the only landscape it sees all day every day. Puppies need new experiences on a regular basis—the opportunity to see, hear, and smell new things; otherwise, the yard soon seems like a prison. What is more, a puppy or dog that is closed in a yard or run simply does not exercise on its own. It must be taken out and walked or played with in order to get enough daily activity.

Daily exercise requirements vary greatly for different breeds of dogs. In general, the sporting and working dogs need a great deal of daily exercise—at least one or two hours of vigorous activity per day. Terriers, too, are very active and, depending on their size, need a lot of exercise so that they won't become "hyper." Size does dictate in part how much exercise a puppy needs on a daily basis. A tiny toy is worn out by a brisk walk around the block, while a giant Newfoundland can go for several miles without feeling a bit tired. To find out about the exercise requirements of your particular breed of puppy, check with your breeder, a breed club, or your veterinarian, or buy one of the booklets about your particular breed, usually available in pet stores.

Play can be part of your exercise routine with your puppy. Some puppies are extremely playful and need no encouragement to chase and fetch a ball or stick, or run and romp around with you in the yard. Others seem to be born sedate and may not enjoy rough-and-tumble activities. You are the best judge of what your puppy likes to do for fun but, whatever it is, you should encourage your puppy to romp and play as much as possible. It is not only good for your puppy but gives you a good chance to teach it some important lessons while interacting with it in a relaxed way. Toss and fetch is an extremely good game for a puppy that enjoys it. It teaches the puppy that it must relinquish the object it has fetched in order for the game to continue. Never allow a puppy to growl or become aggressive in any way while playing. If this should happen, stop the game immediately, scold the puppy and, if necessary, perform the dominance-gentling routine described on page 146.

Keeping a Record

It is always a good idea to keep your own records of your puppy's growth, immunizations, and so forth. Your own records can be very helpful if you move, change veterinarians, or simply want to look up something later on in your puppy's life.

It can be fun to prepare an attractive notebook or card file for your puppy. Children especially may enjoy doing this. Your records do not need to be at all fancy as long as they are accurate and up to date. The following pages have some suggestions of topics that you may want to include in your puppy's record book.

Sample Puppy Record Book

BACKGROUND AND BIRTH RECORD

Breed: _____ Name: _____

Date and place of birth: _____

Where and from whom obtained: _____

Sire and dam: _____
_____

Date obtained: _____

Physical Description of Puppy

    Color: _____

    Markings: _____

    Height: _____

    Weight: _____

    Other outstanding characteristics: _____
_____

Why you chose this puppy: _____

VETERINARIAN

Name: _____

Address: _____

Telephone: _____

Office hours: _____ Call-in times: _____

Emergency telephone: _____

Other nearby veterinarians and/or veterinary hospitals:

_____

Poison control center telephone: _____

MEDICAL RECORDS

First Visit to the Veterinarian

Date: _____ Age of puppy: _____

Veterinarian's comments/suggestions: _____

_____

_____

_____

Record of Immunizations

	1st	2nd	3rd	4th	More
Parvovirus	___	___	___	___	___
Dis-temper(DHL)	___	___	___	___	___
Parainfluenza (CPI)	___	___	___	___	___
Hepatitis (DHL)	___	___	___	___	___
Leptospirosis (DHL)	___	___	___	___	___
Rabies	___	___	___	___	___
Heartworm Test	___	___	___	___	___

Record of Stool Sample Evaluation

Date performed: _____ Result: _____

Dewormings

Dates performed: _____

Next appointment: _____

Other medical information that may be included:
  Date of neutering
  Annual booster shot and heartworm test record
  Other medical or surgical procedures
  Medications given
  Record of illnesses and/or accidents
  Allergies
  Parasite control

GROWTH RECORD

On this page you can record your puppy's weight and height at various regular intervals.

FEEDING RECORD

Puppy's First Diet

    Kind/brand of food: _____

    Amount given: _____ Times per day: _____

Introduction of New Food

    Kind/brand: _____

    Amount given: _____ Times per day: _____

    Puppy's reaction: _____

Date when feedings cut back to

    three times/day: _____

    twice/day: _____

    once/day: _____

Favorite food: _____ Favorite treat: _____

TRAINING RECORD

On this page you can record information about your puppy's housebreaking experiences, when it learned its name, had its first lessons in obedience, attended puppy obedience school and adult obedience school.

Additional Pages or Sections

Depending on how complete you want your puppy's record to be, you can also include sections on the following: Exercise and Play—Favorite Games and Toys; Other Animals in the Household and Your Puppy's Relationship to Them; Grooming—Professional Groomer; Boarding Experiences; Travel With Your Puppy; and any other information that will make your puppy's record book complete. You may also want to leave blank pages for photographs of your puppy at various stages in its life.

5

A Look at Puppy Behavior

In order to understand puppy behavior in general and what makes your own puppy tick in particular, you should know a bit about canine behavior as it has evolved over the years. If you are aware of what constitutes natural, instinctive behavior in dogs, you will be better equipped to work with your puppy rather than fighting it, one of the keys to success. Another key to success in a dog-owner relationship is to recognize that every dog is an individual, the product of a particular set of inherited traits and of early experiences. You cannot expect your puppy to fit into a ready-made mold, and you will cause yourself and your pet a great deal of unhappiness if you try. A final and important factor to recognize is that your own influence has a tremendous impact on your puppy's ultimate behavior.

Canine Behavior

Dogs have developed over the years in the wild as pack animals. This means that they are social in that they rely on other members of the pack for survival and for companionship. They cooperate in hunting for food and often share that food with other pack members, they share in the rearing and protection of young when necessary, and they provide one another with warmth and company. A dog in the wild is never far from its pack members and can always reach them by "calling" if it becomes separated temporarily.

If you realize that your puppy has been born with this ingrown pack mentality, you will be able to understand more about its behavior.

SOCIAL BEHAVIOR

A puppy craves and needs a lot of social interaction with other living beings—humans, other companion animals, and preferably both. Many behavior problems that occur when a puppy is brought into a household stem from loneliness, boredom, and anxiety at suddenly finding itself all alone. Several of these problems and their possible solutions are discussed throughout this book in *Detailed Discussions*. But it is important for you to realize right from the beginning that when a puppy barks excessively, is destructive, chews things it shouldn't, or soils in the house, it is not being consciously "bad" but may be lonely and miserable, or confused because it does not yet understand what you want.

DOMINANCE/SUBMISSION

In the pack there is always a leader and a hierarchy of dominance down to the most submissive animal. Many owner-puppy problems arise from a failure to realize that if yours is a dominant puppy (which was established while the puppy was still with the litter), you must immediately settle that you are its leader; otherwise, the puppy will try to dominate you. If your puppy challenges your authority or acts aggressively in any way, you should immediately perform the dominance-gentling routine described on page 146. Never hurt or frighten your puppy but always act swiftly and firmly whenever it tries to defy you. In a short time the puppy will accept that you are its leader and usually will not challenge your authority again. If at some later date your puppy does decide to challenge your authority, you simply have to immediately repeat the dominance-gentling.

If, on the other hand, you have a submissive puppy that immediately lies down and rolls over on its back the minute you approach it, you have to be very careful not to be too harsh with it or you will frighten it, causing it to become timid and resort to fear biting and/or fear urination.

Of course there are gradations in between these two extremes, and you have to govern your actions according to your own puppy's temperament.

AGGRESSION

Three primary kinds of aggression occur in pet dogs: active aggression aimed at a human who encroaches on what a dog considers its territory or possessions; reactive aggression aimed at a human that stems from fear of being touched, moved, or even approached and is often the result of overly harsh treatment of a timid puppy; and aggression toward other pets (usually dogs) either in the home or outdoors. Even within the cooperative pack there is some aggression among dogs, either to establish or reestablish dominance over another pack member, out of fear of another pack member, or to protect food, nest, young, or a mate from another pack member.

When dogs live with humans as pets, additional factors may contribute to aggression and inter-dog aggression. Fear-induced aggression may be avoided by recognizing that a puppy is overly timid and fearful when you first get it and socializing it very carefully, gradually accustoming it to new people and situations. If a puppy has a genetic propensity toward fearful aggression, it may require more ongoing vigilance and socialization. With a puppy like this, you may need to socialize it on a regular basis for the rest of its life, continuously reinforcing good, nonaggressive behavior and being constantly alert to situations the puppy may find threatening and react to in an aggressive manner. Later on in this chapter you can read about how an owner's own (often unrecognized) aggressiveness can contribute to a puppy's becoming an aggressive dog.

TERRITORIALITY

Within the pack, each family group usually has its own "turf," the nest area where young are raised and the family unit goes to rest. Adult pack members respect other families' territorial boundaries. The pack as a whole, too, has its larger turf, marked off by male members in urine and continuously patrolled by them to ensure that no alien nonpack member encroaches.

Some dog breeds (terriers, in particular) are naturally more territorial than others, and you have to be careful not to foster territorial behavior in a puppy. Overterritoriality can lead to aggression (toward both humans and other dogs), excessive barking, and roaming and urine marking by uncastrated males. Never allow your puppy to get away with declaring that any thing or place belongs to it.

OTHER BEHAVIOR

These are the primary types of natural dog behavior you have to learn how to work with in a puppy. Sexual behavior will not surface for a while, and in a pet dog most of the troubling behaviors that result from the sexual drive can be resolved by early neutering of both males and females.

Table 13 summarizes some behavior traits that may cause problems and how best to deal with them.

Handling a Puppy

Once you realize that your puppy has certain inherent behavior traits, the trick is to work with these traits and enhance their positive aspects. Your puppy will form habits early, and you might as well make them good habits from the beginning. Problems can arise if you allow undesirable behavior to become a habit; then you will have to go through a lengthy process to undo it.

If you think a little ahead, you will realize that certain behaviors that seem "cute" to you and your family when your puppy is small may soon become annoying habits as it grows. This does not mean you should be constantly correcting your puppy and jumping on it for every little thing it does, but it does mean that you need to use common sense and consistency and anticipate a bit.

Do not be harsh with a puppy, however. You will never teach a puppy anything but distrust by inflicting pain or by frightening it. Puppies do chew, wet, bark, jump up on people and things, and so forth. That's natural. In order for a puppy to learn that this behavior is not acceptable, you have to teach it. A puppy has no possible way of knowing what it is you want it to do or not do if you don't

Table 13 *Puppy Behavior Traits That May Cause Problems,
Their Manifestations and Possible Solutions*

Trait	Problems	Manifestations	Possible Solutions
Sociability	Boredom, loneliness	Destructive behavior—chewing, digging; escaping, roaming	Another pet*; more exercise, play, novelty
	Anxiety at separation from humans	Barking, whining, soiling, destructive behavior	Condition to human absence and boarding*
Territoriality	"Guarding" behavior	Excessive barking, growling, aggression	Desensitize; avoid "Negative Reinforcement"*
		Inappropriate elimination ("marking")	Neuter
Dominance	Aggression toward other dogs	Growling, fighting	Desensitize; avoid "Negative Reinforcement"*
	Aggression toward humans	Growling, biting	Dominance—gentling†; avoid aggressive play
Fear	Apprehension with new animals/people/situations	Growling, biting, cringing, inappropriate elimination, trembling, phobias	Early Socialization*; avoid harsh treatment

*See *Detailed Discussion*.   †See page 146.

89

show it patiently and repeatedly, and praise it when it acts correctly. More about reward and punishment later on.

Learn to work with your puppy's natural curiosity and friendliness. For instance, if you start when a puppy is very young to teach it to come when called, you will be working *with* its natural eagerness to run to you all the time. If you wait until the puppy is older and more independent, you may have a battle of wills on your hands. In Part Two of this book we will talk about various ways to work within a puppy's natural stages of development. But common sense should tell you that if you can make a natural action into a good habit when a puppy is young, you are many steps ahead of the game.

Be careful not to allow your puppy to train you, however. This is a trap that is all too easy to fall into. It won't take long for a puppy to learn that if it whines piteously, for instance, you will come quickly and pay attention to it; or if it wags its tail and looks at you beseechingly, you will give it a food treat. Once you allow a puppy to make you do what it wants, it won't be long before it will expect you to give in to its every demand, and you will be waiting on it hand and foot.

The single most important aspect of successful puppy handling is *socialization*. This is an umbrella term that we use throughout this book to describe the process of accustoming a puppy to the world around it—to people, things, experiences, and places. If a puppy is exposed to a wide variety of sensations, and perceptions early in its life and learns to accept them and how to react to them, it will be prepared for just about anything that happens in the course of its lifetime and will be equipped to behave properly wherever it is. Don't make the mistake of assuming that just because you live miles out in the country your puppy will never have to walk on a leash, for instance. Or, just because you have a family of ten your puppy will never need to be boarded in a kennel. Circumstances do change, emergencies do come up, and special occasions arise. Every puppy should learn the basics of certain kinds of behavior and become comfortable in a number of different situations. If you expose your puppy early in life to all the experiences we talk about in this book (and any others that you think may arise in your household), you should never have to deal with a recalcitrant older dog, nor will the dog be traumatized by a totally new experience.

*How Your Temperament Can Affect Your Puppy's Behavior**

One of the interesting factors that we have discovered in our treatment of behavior problems in pets is that an owner's own personality and temperament often inadvertently affect a dog's behavior. In some cases the influence is direct, and in others a more subtle message is conveyed to a puppy.

Although we do not have the space to go into all of the ramifications of owner-dog interaction or to discuss the entire spectrum of owner personalities, we will talk about two types of owners and the possible influences they may have on their puppies' ultimate behavior. These examples may help you to recognize the importance of the messages you give to your puppy, both directly and indirectly.

AGGRESSIVE OWNERS

Aggressive owners tend to have problems with aggression in their dogs. They also have a preference for large or feisty male dogs and very often do not consider cas-

* Based on: Hamilton, G. and M. J. Robbins, "Psychology of the Owner Factor in Animal Behavior." American Hospital Association (AAHA), 48th Annual Meeting: Scientific Presentations, 1981.

trating their pets, thus compounding the problem. Their dogs often become aggressive toward humans, but they also may show aggression toward other dogs (usually other males).

If you recognize that you (or another family member) have a streak of hostility or repressed anger in your nature, you have to be very careful not to transmit this to your puppy. If you encourage a puppy to indulge in aggressive play (tug-of-war, for example), praise it when it growls at or threatens another animal or unknown human, "sic" it on cats or wildlife, you are giving it a clear message that you want it to be aggressive. The message may be more subtle, however, and not conveyed by direct encouragement but by tacit approval of or disregard of the puppy's aggressiveness. If you allow your puppy to get away with aggression in any form without immediately correcting it by dominance-gentling or stopping it verbally, you are conveying approval of its aggression. You should then be neither surprised nor angry when your puppy grows up to be an aggressive dog.

INDULGENT OWNERS

Indulgent owners are those who cannot set or maintain any clear rules with their puppies. They tend to have a lot of animals and to care a great deal about their pets. The problem is that the pets usually develop a number of behavior problems—unruliness, house soiling, and even aggression.

If you or your family tend to be a bit undisciplined and believe that a puppy will learn how to behave simply by being well loved, you are letting yourself in for a problem adult dog. If you realize this tendency in yourself, make a real effort to overcome the inclination to let your puppy rule the roost. As we pointed out above, a puppy has no way of knowing how to behave unless you show it. Appropriate discipline and setting of limits provide security and a *real* sense of love to a puppy. You are not doing your puppy a favor by letting it grow up with no idea of acceptable behavior; it will grow up to be an obnoxious dog. Further, if you have a dominant puppy, you run the risk of allowing it to become an aggressive dog by never assuming a leadership role over it.

Think about the kind of dog you would like your puppy to grow up to be, and then try to be honest with yourself, recognizing if you have a tendency to influence your puppy's behavior in a negative way. If you can do this and adjust your handling of your puppy positively, you will be well on your way to avoiding future behavior problems.

Discipline: Reward and Punishment

Clarity, flexibility, affection, firmness, consistency, repetition, and a commonsense approach—these are the tools of successful puppy discipline. If a puppy learns early in life that you are its leader, it will want to please you, gain your approval, and follow your instructions. If, on the other hand, your puppy learns early in life to fear and distrust you, or senses your lack of consistency, it will ignore you when possible and/or try to bully you into allowing it to have its own way. Always follow up when you give your puppy a command. Give the command once, and if the puppy does not respond, enforce the command.

You must start out in the owner-puppy relationship with the clear understanding that you are the owner and it is the puppy. When you first own a puppy, it is small, helpless, completely dependent on you for its physical well-being, and quite malleable. This is the time to begin to teach it how you want it to behave. If you wait until the puppy becomes physically stronger, independent, and feisty, you will have a much more difficult time. If you start when the puppy is young, and you are firm, consistent, and clear in your instructions, you will never have to resort to any kind of harsh discipline. In most cases the resulting adult dog will always be well mannered, with little or no effort required on your part.

REINFORCEMENT

That is not to say that even a generally well-behaved puppy or older dog may not sometimes seem to forget a previously learned lesson or perhaps get it into its head to test you a bit to see if you really meant what you said. Feisty, naturally assertive puppies may do this often, and there is usually a stage around six or seven months of age when most puppies go through a rebellious "teenage" period. They are also apt to challenge your authority again when they are around a year old.

You should try to be alert to these backsliding incidents, no matter how minor, and immediately nip them in the bud with appropriate actions, reinforcing your earlier lessons.

You should also continuously reinforce your puppy's good behavior in a positive manner. Always praise your dog when it behaves well in any situation. Remind it regularly and often that you are pleased with it and that it is a "good dog." Your approval is your puppy's best reward and its most compelling reason for good behavior. (See *Positive Reinforcement*, page 213).

PROVIDING ALTERNATIVES

One of the most useful tools in teaching a puppy to redirect normal behavior in an appropriate way is to provide an alternative. If you give your puppy an acceptable alternative for an action or behavior you do not want it to indulge in, it takes no time at all for the puppy to understand what you want. Thus, when the puppy starts to chew on something unacceptable, give it a chew toy; when it begins to eliminate in an inappropriate place, immediately take it to the nearest appropriate place. In other words, redirect the puppy to an appropriate way of behaving. If you can do this each and every time the puppy indulges in an unacceptable behavior, it soon gets the message.

By the way, do not offer an alternative at the same time that you scold the puppy for the unwanted action. If you say "No" at the same time that you offer a substitute, the puppy gets the conflicting message that the alternative is not any more acceptable than the original act. Although this may appear to be common sense, it is a mistake that is easy to make without thinking.

REWARDS

If yours is a very devoted, anxious-to-please puppy, your approval may possibly be the only reward necessary for good behavior. If, on the other hand, your puppy tends to be a bit independent, is easily distracted and very active, you may need to use a food treat to reward it, at least in the initial stages of teaching. Always combine a pat or a hug and a "good dog" with a biscuit so that your puppy knows that your affection and approval have been earned as well as a tasty morsel. Then, as your puppy becomes more responsive to your wishes and voice commands, you can gradually remove the food treat as an incentive and let your affectionate approval be the puppy's only reward.

It is important to replace food treats as a puppy's reward for good behavior before they become part and parcel of every daily action. You will soon have a very fat puppy on your hands if you allow this to happen. What is more, a puppy should never feel that it has earned a food treat just for acting normal and well behaved. Of course, you can give food treats on occasion—when the puppy has been particularly good, learned something new, been especially cute, or just because you love it—but try not to overdo it.

While we're on the topic of overdoing food treats, the question may occur: Can you spoil a puppy? Yes and no. You cannot possibly spoil a puppy by loving it and giving it a lot of affection and praise when it is good. But, as we said above, you can spoil it by giving in to its every whim, whether it is good or not. A puppy that is allowed to do anything it wants and is still praised, petted, fed treats, and given approval will turn into a spoiled dog that is not very pleasant to have around. So, temper your approval and affection a bit and let them be rewards for your puppy's good behavior, not simply for its very existence.

PUNISHMENT

As we said before, harsh punishment is never constructive when dealing with a puppy. There almost certainly will be times, however, when you will have to let your puppy know that it has misbehaved, and a harsh look probably will not do the trick.

Some puppies are so sensitive to their owners—so "tuned in," so to speak—that simple disapproval is sufficient punishment. A "bad dog" accompanied by a scowl and disappointed head shake may be enough for this type of puppy in many circumstances.

For most high-spirited puppies, however, the message may have to be more pointed. You may need to be quite firm and forceful with a stubborn or hyperactive puppy. By this we mean *verbally* forceful, never physically abusive or frightening. Do not allow your temper to take over, no matter what the infraction. Never yell or shout at a puppy; you will only confuse and frighten it. Take a few deep breaths and count to ten, even if your pet has just broken your grandmother's vase or knocked the bud off your prize rose.

Never call a puppy to you to be scolded, or it will learn not to come when called. Go and get the puppy, take it to the scene of the infraction, and then scold. This lets it know clearly just what it is being scolded for and reminds it of its actions. The old theory about not scolding a puppy for an infraction that occurred some time ago simply does not hold true. You would not neglect to praise a puppy that has behaved well during your absence by taking it over to the newspapers it has used, for example, and telling it what a "good dog" it was.

By the same token, appropriate scolding can be effective in a similar time frame. If a puppy has chewed something while you were out, it is never too late to scold it. If you take the puppy to the spot of the chewing and then scold, the puppy will have no doubt what it is you are scolding it for. If, on the other hand, you let the puppy get away with the chewing, it will naturally assume that it was all right to do.

One of the best punishments is one that a puppy brings on itself. If it begins to chew an object and is greeted with a vile taste, it learns a valuable lesson and will not want to chew that object or another one like it in the near or hopefully distant future. This is an excellent learning tool and one that you can utilize in a number of ways again and again. Let the puppy learn that certain actions result in unpleasant experiences. We will give specifics of this as we go along.

OBEDIENCE TRAINING

We are strongly in favor of obedience training for all puppies, beginning as early as possible. Puppy obedience school, or at-home obedience lessons if your puppy is not yet fully immunized (ask your veterinarian about this), should begin no later than ten weeks of age. By going to obedience class you will learn how to control your puppy properly and how to convey what it is you want through clear instructions and actions. Your puppy will learn to understand exactly what it is you are conveying to it.

Once you have accomplished this you will have a valuable tool at your disposal that you can use again and again in all kinds of situations and places. Your puppy or older dog need never be confused about what you want it to do, and you will never have to resort to punishment in order to control your pet. We will talk more about obedience training in Chapters 8 and 11.

PART TWO

One Month
at a Time

NOTE:
ABOUT THE FOLLOWING CHAPTERS

The tables and descriptions contained in the following
chapters that describe a puppy's development are based on
the *average* puppy.

You should bear in mind that each individual puppy var-
ies somewhat in its physical development and emotional
and behavioral maturity. The size and breed of your puppy
also affects its rate of physical and behavioral growth. A
tiny toy, for example, becomes sexually mature at about
six months of age and reaches behavioral adulthood when
it is somewhere around a year old. At the other end of the
spectrum, a slow developer such as a bearded collie or a
giant Irish wolfhound isn't sexually mature until it is
somewhere around a year and a half old, and attains full
physical and behavioral maturity only when it is two to
three years old.

Therefore, you should take the information that follows
in the context of your own puppy's natural growth rate,
and remember that its various levels and stages of devel-

opment may not necessarily be reached at the exact times indicated. They usually occur in the given sequence, however, and you should follow the socialization and training steps in the time frames that are indicated.

6

Birth to Six Weeks: From Helpless Infant to Toddler

We have expanded this chapter from one month to the first six weeks in a puppy's life because these are the weeks almost all puppies are with their dams, in the care of their breeders. During this very important time a puppy develops from a completely helpless, dependent infant into a toddling youngster that is almost ready to venture out into the world.

Although you will have little, if anything, to do with your puppy's well-being during these early weeks of its life, you may want to know something about the stages it goes through and just what constitutes good care on the part of the breeder. As we emphasized in *Choosing a Source* (page 22), the breeder's early handling of a puppy has a great deal to do with starting it off on the right foot. If you have already selected a breeder and live near enough, you may be able to visit the litter from time to time during these early weeks of life and observe for yourself just how the puppies are developing.

Table 14 HIGHLIGHTS CHART

Birth to Six Weeks: From Helpless Infant to Toddler

	PUPPY DEVELOPMENT		BREEDER INVOLVEMENT	
	Physical	**Social/Behavioral**	**Puppy's Health/ Safety Needs**	**Working with Puppy Readiness**
Birth to Two Weeks	Crawls Sucks Needs maternal stimulation to urinate/defecate	Completely dependent on mother Sleeps most of the time	Mother and littermates for warmth; proper environmental temperature; clean, dry nest Maintain dam's good health/nutrition Be sure each puppy gets to nurse enough; supplement if necessary	Human contact important
Two to Three Weeks	Can hear Eyes open Baby teeth begin to erupt Can stand Eliminates alone Can lap liquid	Begins to interact with littermates	Begin weaning; introduce supplementary liquids	

Table 14 HIGHLIGHTS CHART
Birth to Six Weeks: From Helpless Infant to Toddler (Cont.)

	PUPPY DEVELOPMENT		BREEDER INVOLVEMENT	
	Physical	Social/Behavioral	Puppy's Health/ Safety Needs	Working with Puppy Readiness
Three to Four Weeks	Starts to explore Can eat soft food Begins to walk	Begins socialization with littermates; bites, paws, barks; very aware of environment	Introduce solid food	Expose to sounds and obstacles; provide external stimulation Still needs security of mother and littermates
Four to Five Weeks	Walks a little	Plays with littermates; chases, pounces Reacts to noises Aware of people	4 meals/day; nurse at night Separate from mother for short periods	Continue aural and visual stimulation Needs playtime Continue human contact Introduce to steps
Five to Six Weeks		Exhibits curiosity and fearlessness	Begin immunizations†	Begin Socialization*

* See *Detailed Discussion*.   † See Chapter 4.

The Dam and Sire

The single most important factor in the birth of a healthy litter of puppies is the soundness of both parents. A responsible breeder will be sure that the dam is in excellent physical and emotional health before she is bred and will not breed her until she is physically and behaviorally mature, usually not before her second heat season. Before breeding, both the dam and sire should have been immunized, dewormed, and examined thoroughly for any possible genetic faults. This may include pelvic X rays for signs of hip dysplasia if the breed is prone to this disorder.

The disposition of the parents is also very important; both should be happy, outgoing, and even-tempered. This is why we suggest that prospective owners meet both dam and sire if possible before making a final decision on a puppy.

Quality nutrition is essential for the dam during gestation and especially during lactation, when her energy requirements are extremely high. She will need up to three times her normal amount of food in order to produce sufficient milk for her puppies. Most breeders divide the dam's daily intake into several meals a day during this time.

The First Three Weeks

The first three weeks in a puppy's life are a critical period. During this neonatal period a puppy is completely dependent on its mother and littermates for food and warmth. It sleeps almost all of the time that it is not actively nursing. This is essential so that its still undeveloped neurological and muscular systems begin to mature. It may crawl around a bit but soon returns to its mother.

In general, the puppies should be disturbed as little as possible for the first two weeks. Many dams make it very clear that they want to be left entirely alone with their puppies during this time, while others crave company and do not object to an occasional well-known visitor or to a family member picking up a puppy. If it does not make the dam nervous, most puppies respond to gentle stroking and caressing after the first week or so. Outsiders should not be allowed to touch or handle the puppies, however. During this period the primary responsibilities of the breeder are to make sure that the litter stays dry, clean, and warm. Although the dam licks the puppies to stimulate urination and defecation and keep them clean, the lining of the whelping box may need to be changed frequently in order to keep it clean and dry. Usually, sufficient warmth is generated by body heat from the dam and littermates, but the whelping box must be kept at an even temperature in order to prevent chilling. Sometimes artificial heat is needed.

Sometime between ten days and two and a half weeks of age a puppy's eyes and ears open, and it is time to begin to accustom it gradually to sights and sounds. Quiet music and soothing speech can set the stage for human interaction, and a variety of faces and shapes help a puppy begin to learn about the world around it.

By three weeks of age a puppy usually is able to stand alone and even take a few wobbly steps. Its baby teeth begin to erupt, and it starts to eliminate without maternal stimulation. It discovers its littermates and may initiate play with them and its mother. Each puppy should now be picked up and handled gently every day in order to become used to human touch, and spoken to regularly.

Three to Six Weeks

At about three to four weeks of age a puppy is ready to learn to lap liquids, and some supplementary gruel-type food can be introduced, although complete weaning should not take place until a puppy is around seven weeks old.

Although a puppy may begin to exhibit some independence and wander off from its mother and siblings a bit, it still needs the security of its dam and littermates most of the time and should be removed from them for only short periods of time. It becomes very aware of people, their arrival and departure, around four to five weeks of age. This is the time to begin serious socialization.

Socialization: The Single Most Important Process in Bringing Up a Happy, Responsive, Satisfactory Puppy

Socialization is the process of accustoming a puppy to all aspects of life with humans in a home setting and of introducing it to a variety of sensory experiences early in life so that it will be able to adapt and respond well to a wide range of relationships and situations. Socialization is extremely important. In recent years responsible dog breeders have become more and more aware of puppies' needs for early socialization and have been providing it.

Even though this concept would seem to be an obvious, commonsense approach to puppy upbringing, many puppy owners apparently find it very mysterious. They believe all that is required in order to raise a happy, responsive pet is to put it in a big fenced-in yard, feed it regularly, and pat it occasionally. Then they are amazed and annoyed when their pet doesn't know how to act in the car, has difficulty accepting strangers, or becomes frightened when they take it into a public place.

If you wait until a dog is an adult, it can still be socialized to new experiences and people, but the process is much more difficult, is often less successful, and is apt to require continuous reinforcement throughout the remainder of a dog's life. Recently, retired racing greyhounds that had spent three to four years living in cages were made available for adoption. These dogs had to spend a lot of time becoming "rehabilitated" (socialized) to life in a home both before and after their adoption; only then were they able to adjust to life with humans outside of their cages. Because of their basically gentle personalities, many of these rehabilitated greyhounds became successful pets, but it required professional help and very patient, devoted owners who were willing and able to take the time to achieve this.

EARLY SOCIALIZATION—BY BREEDERS

The same thing can occur when very young puppies are raised in cages with little if any real contact with humans. They quickly become what has been dubbed "kennel-shy." At best they are unresponsive and indifferent to people; at worst they become timid, nervous, very territorial, and may develop into fear biters.

It is important for a puppy to begin to get used to being handled as soon as it can be taken away from its mother for brief periods of time beginning at two to three weeks of age, but the key period for socialization to humans begins at around four to five weeks of age. When a puppy is able to toddle around a little and is well into weaning, it must be removed from the nest, away from both its mother and littermates, and allowed to spend some time in the company of one or more humans. At this time a puppy's senses of smell, hearing, sight, and feeling are becoming developed, and it needs a wide range of experiences. It should be gently stroked and petted all over its body, be held, and be put down on the floor and allowed to explore seated people. Although a very young puppy should not be exposed to many people at once, it does need to meet and be handled on a regular basis (at least once a day) by several different people of different ages and sexes, if possible.

In the next few weeks, socialization should continue and expand. The puppy should be removed from its nest for longer and longer periods, and should be allowed to explore the environment under strict supervision. If it is being raised in a household, it should be introduced to the normal sights, sounds, and smells of a home. Even in a kennel situation a breeder can expose a puppy to the sounds of a radio, doors closing, feet walking, the feel of different surfaces on its feet, and so on.

At the same time that socialization to the outside world is occurring, interaction with its littermates plays an important part in the development of a puppy. The period from around five to seven or eight weeks is the time when a puppy learns a lot from its siblings. It learns about action and reaction—that if it bites, it is apt to be bitten. It learns just how far it can go with another living creature; how much pain it can inflict and when to stop. During this time it also learns important lessons about dominant and submissive behaviors—what their signals are and how to react to them. So, it is also important for a puppy to remain with its littermates, if possible, during this critical two- to three-week period before adoption. Puppies that are taken away from the litter too young may have to be taught these important lessons by their owners. That is why it is advisable to wait until a puppy is seven or eight weeks old before adopting it. (See also *Nip Aggression in the Bud*, page 146).

Although it is impossible to know exactly how well a puppy has been socialized to the environment when you meet it for the first time at six to eight weeks of age, you can tell a great deal about how it has been accustomed to handling by people. Some of the ways to determine this are outlined in Chapter 3.

110

EARLY SOCIALIZATION—BY OWNERS

As soon as a puppy has had time to adjust to life away from its brothers and sisters and has had time to form new attachments to its owners, it is time to begin to think seriously about its socialization in your home.

Some of the normal steps in socializing a puppy to live in a home situation occur without any planning or thought on your part. Obviously, family members handle, pet, and play with the puppy, and it soon meets and begins to know any other household pets. The puppy hears, sees, tastes, and feels a number of new sensations. Radios, televisions, and stereos play. Doors slam. Cooking aromas, perfumes, soaps and detergents, floor polish, and newsprint are smelled. Carpets, rugs, tile, and linoleum are sat on or slipped across. Salty faces and dirty shoes are licked and chew-sticks and probably some fingers are nibbled and nipped. The puppy may experience cold for the first time and may be exposed to so many new sights that it is saturated with them.

In most households, these things occur as a matter of course. Soon, all these normal, everyday sensations are old hat to your puppy, and it is time to introduce it to a wider world.

Even before your puppy is completely immunized and it is safe to take it abroad in public, it should begin to learn about people outside the family. When friends come over, always include the puppy in the group, at least for a while. Make a point of introducing your pet to anyone who comes to the door. If you live in an isolated area and have few visitors, invite people over to meet your new puppy, and let it meet them. The wider the variety of people that a young puppy meets and learns to accept, the better. One word of caution, however: Early experiences can work in a negative way, too. Don't allow your pet to be frightened by too many people converging on it at once with overly loud voices and overly heavy footsteps or rough handling. Accustoming a small puppy to accept people does not include terrorizing it or "toughening it up." This may only contribute to the development of a fearful dog. Use your common sense and take the puppy (or the people) away if it becomes overtired, overexcited, or at all frightened.

This is the time, too, to get the puppy used to being handled and groomed. Begin immediately to brush and/or comb your pet (depending on its coat), and incorporate a thorough allover hand examination into each grooming session. Areas that are particularly sensitive can quickly become "no touch" places if you don't insist on handling them regularly and gently. These include feet and foot pads, ears (both the pinnae and the areas around the ear openings), around the eyes, mouth and teeth, stomach, and around the anus. If your puppy learns to trust you early in life, you will be able to examine and treat any part of its body without any problems later on if it should become necessary. Be sure not to pinch or hurt; again, this is a negative lesson.

Another sensation that your puppy should become accustomed to right away is wearing a collar and leash. This is discussed in more detail in *Accustom Your Puppy to Wearing a Collar and Leash*, page 151.

It is never too early after you get a puppy for it to begin to learn *Car Manners* (see page 155), even if the only place it can safely go until it is protected from disease is the veterinarian's office or for a short ride around the block.

Along with these various kinds of socialization to physical experiences, your puppy should also begin to learn how to behave in different situations. First and foremost, it can be taught to respond to its name (see *Puppy Obedience: Verbal Commands*, page 134), can begin to learn about where to eliminate, not to chew and bite anything but its toys, not to be aggressive, and so forth. All of these important behaviors should begin to be ingrained in a positive way as soon as you get your puppy.

CONTINUING SOCIALIZATION

As your puppy gets older and is able to get out in the world, all of the experiences and behaviors that you have introduced should be continuously reinforced (see *Positive Reinforcement*, page 213). Serious obedience training (Chapter 11) should begin as early as possible, as well as professional grooming, if it will be necessary. Your puppy should learn to stay away from home, continue to meet new people and other animals, and have new experiences.

Take your pet with you as much as possible after it is immunized for long walks in the country or on city sidewalks, into malls or marketplaces (if dogs are allowed), in crowds, and to areas where other dogs are found. Don't give in to the temptation to leave it at home closed in the house or in a run or yard, even though it may seem easier. The earlier a puppy is accustomed to accepting new situations and experiences and behaving well in them, the better off both of you will be when the necessity arises (and it certainly will) to take your dog into a public place among strange people and/or dogs.

If there are special situations such as travel or showing that you know your dog will be experiencing, start it off on short trips as early as possible.

As we have said throughout this book, common sense is the best approach to intelligent puppy raising, just as it is in raising a child. Introducing a puppy to the world around it and helping it to learn how to behave early in its life will allow it to become a well-rounded adult dog that is able to cope with whatever comes up in a calm, well-behaved fashion. It will also help to avoid fears and behavior problems later on.

By the fifth week of age a puppy can be removed from the nest more often for frequent, short play and exploring sessions. Its muscles and coordination have developed quite a bit, and this is a good time to begin to acquaint it with obstacles and to teach it how to negotiate stairs. Constant supervision is important, however, as a puppy of this age may have more curiosity than sense. It is still important to guard a puppy against sudden changes in environmental temperature and protect it against drafts. As soon as a puppy appears to tire, it should be put back in its nest.

A puppy is able to eat soft solid food quite well by now. It should, however, be returned to its dam after each meal, and puppies and dam should sleep together at night. At this stage the puppies nurse at least once a day, at night. Gradually, the dam's milk starts to diminish, and she plays a large part in the final weaning process, pushing the puppies away when she has no more milk to give them.

At about this time, the veterinarian usually begins the puppy's immunization series. We discuss immunizations in detail in Chapter 4.

7

Six to Eight Weeks:
A Lot of Growing Up

This two-week period is one of great importance in a puppy's social and behavioral development. Although there is a gradual slowing down from the extremely rapid and dramatic physical changes that a puppy has gone through in the first six weeks of life, there is still a lot of growing up to do before a puppy is ready to venture out into the world on its own.

This is a transitional period during which a puppy needs interaction with its littermates as well as continued human handling and socialization in order to develop into a well-rounded pet. This is when each puppy develops more fully into an individual and gains self-confidence and also a sense of limits within the safe framework of the litter. Too-early adoption and removal from the give-and-take of sibling interplay robs a puppy of an important step in its behavioral development and may result in future behavior problems, as we will discuss later on in this and future chapters.

Table 15 HIGHLIGHTS CHART
Six to Eight Weeks: A Lot of Growing Up

| | PUPPY DEVELOPMENT | | BREEDER OR OWNER INVOLVEMENT | |
	Physical	**Social/Behavioral**	**Puppy's Health/ Safety Needs**	**Working with Puppy Readiness**
Six to Seven Weeks	Well coordinated	Investigates	Protect from harm	Provide supervised freedom to explore
	Hearing and sight fully developed	Engages in sexual play Tests limits in playfighting with littermates	Avoid slippery surfaces	Continue Socialization* Environmental stimulation very important— exploration Human contact very important; play
Seven to Eight Weeks	Full compliment of baby teeth (28)	Begins to be more cautious, less reckless, but still very curious	Protect from physical harm—Space Management*	If still with litter, should spend most of time away from mother
		Begins to eliminate away from nest area	Weaning completed; 4 meals/day†	New Home; lay the groundwork for Errorless Housebreaking*

* See *Detailed Discussion.*   † See Chapter 4.

Six Weeks Old

At about six weeks of age a puppy is quite well coordinated. It can see and hear, and is quite steady on its feet. Almost completely weaned from its mother, a six-week-old puppy is beginning to feel very independent and is physically able to engage in a lot of investigative activity.

Human caretakers need to be aware of a puppy's rapidly increasing physical capacities and protect it from harm. Little legs will reach further, and the original enclosure or pen may not have high enough sides anymore. If possible, the litter's space should be enlarged to allow the puppies to explore and run around more while still contained in a safe environment. It is very important at this stage to be sure that floors are not slick or slippery. Puppy bones are very soft and can be easily bruised or broken if a puppy slips in headlong romping; indoor-outdoor carpet tiles covered with newspaper, for example, can protect puppies from accidental injury.

The puppies enjoy new objects to look at and climb on: A sturdy cardboard box, stuffed toy, or large beach ball can provide hours of entertainment for a litter of puppies. Remember that the puppy's sharp little teeth are almost all in now, however, and any object that is left in their area when they are unsupervised should be puppy-proof so that small bits of pieces cannot be chewed off and swallowed.

Each puppy needs time alone with a human or humans, away from the litter, and should be provided with at least one period a day of individual activity. A short playtime or romp with a human is a very good learning experience for a puppy. Most puppies will follow a human around at this stage, and a puppy can be allowed to wander from room to room, exploring, as long as it is continuously supervised and never left alone in any room that has not been completely puppy-proofed. (See *Space Management*, page 32).

This is also a good time to introduce a puppy to other objects and areas in a home. The puppy can be picked up and shown objects that are at human eye level—mirrors and windows, for example. It can be taught how to negotiate doors and stairs, and so forth. If a puppy is not familiarized with a normal household by the breeder, you will have to perform this aspect of socialization after you adopt your puppy.

Whether or not it is possible for a breeder to introduce a puppy to household experiences, it is essential that a puppy become increasingly socialized to humans at this stage. The puppies should be spoken to regularly and exposed to as many different people as possible. In *Judging Behavior*, page 45, we talk about ways to determine whether or not this important aspect of socialization has been performed.

Puppies this age play with their littermates all the time. It is in the give-and-take of play-fighting with littermates that a puppy learns the limits of aggressive behavior. It learns how far it can go without retaliation: how hard it can bite without being bitten back and how roughly it can play before a sibling turns around and hurts it back. This is why we counsel so strongly against too-early adoption of a puppy. Without this valuable lesson in limits, a puppy has no sense of its own ability to inflict pain, nor can it learn the valuable pack lesson in dominant/submissive behavior signals. As we discuss in *Socialization*, page 108, and in *Nip Aggression in the Bud*, page 146, you then have to teach your puppy these lessons.

Seven Weeks Old

At this age a puppy is almost ready to leave its canine family. It continues to develop socially and needs even more opportunities to grow in experiences and relationships with people. Weaning should be all but complete. A full set of baby teeth are now in place, and a puppy should be eating solid food. It should spend almost all of its time except at night away from its dam—with littermates or with humans.

At this stage most puppies begin to eliminate in an area away from their sleeping spot, if there is room in their enclosure. If the puppies are being brought up in a household, a breeder may now begin to lay the groundwork for errorless housebreaking.

Errorless Housebreaking

Because so many puppy owners do not know how to go about housebreaking properly, they find it time-consuming, frustrating, and difficult. It probably is also the area of puppy behavior in which there is the least success and the greatest amount of recidivism. This seems to be especially true with small dogs.

Owners often simply give up and either live with the problem (and mess) or allow the dog to train them. A well-trained owner may arrange her entire work and recreation schedule around her puppy's elimination needs and worries constantly that she may not arrive home "on time."

Others expect a dog to be able to ignore a legitimate need and wait for excessively long periods of time without relieving itself. Some people resort to all kinds of artificial means to accomplish this: withholding water, for example, or closing a puppy in a small cage in the mistaken belief that it will never soil its sleeping quarters. Our answer to that is, "How would you feel if somebody locked you out of the bathroom all day?"

119

These methods are not only cruel but may create abnormal neurotic behavior as well as being useless. If a puppy really needs to go badly, it will go wherever it is.

When you attempt to mold a dog's elimination needs into a schedule that is acceptable to you, it results in nothing but guilt—yours or your pet's, or both. This is totally unnecessary if you follow the method outlined below. You should be able to stay out late on occasion without worrying about your dog's well-being, and at the same time the dog should be able to relieve itself in an acceptable place when this happens.

An acceptable alternative in the house will also stand you and your dog in good stead in case of illness or other unexpected circumstances. If you are ill and cannot take your dog outdoors, or there is a blizzard and you can't get the door open until you dress and shovel, your dog will have a place to go. If the dog is ill and has diarrhea, or becomes somewhat incontinent when it is elderly, it will also have a place where it can eliminate in your absence without feeling guilty or upset.

A GOOD BEGINNING

Although a puppy's sphincter muscles are not fully developed until it is at least ten weeks old and you cannot expect any control over elimination until then, you can start your puppy off on the right foot as soon as you get it.

In *Space Management*, page 32, we mentioned lining a puppy's entire room with newspapers. The reason for this is twofold: it will protect your floor, but more important it will accustom your puppy to relieving itself on paper. A puppy can develop a liking for the feel of a particular surface underfoot when it relieves itself, and if it doesn't become used to wood or carpet or tile, it will not connect the feeling of those surfaces with the act of urinating or defecating. Indoors, newspaper will be all that it becomes used to.

If you live in an area where your puppy can be outdoors in your own yard without being exposed to other dogs or their waste, you can also immediately begin to take it outside. Don't expect it to understand that it is meant to relieve itself outdoors until it is ready to exercise some control. There is no harm in praising it if it does, however.

Many people make a big fuss about diet as a factor in housebreaking. Of course, if a puppy has constant diarrhea due to a sudden change in diet or because of illness, it is useless to try to get it to wait. But if there are papers on the entire floor, the puppy will not be learning bad habits while you solve its intestinal problems. Otherwise diet, per se, has little to do with success in housebreaking.

STEP TWO

After a week or two you will probably notice that your puppy tends to use one area of its space for elimination. This may be a pretty large segment at first. Remove the papers from the half of the room not being used to eliminate on. This bare part should be the side with the food, water, and bedding. Your puppy will almost always continue to use the papered area for elimination. If it begins to go elsewhere in the room you have moved too quickly. Put the papers back. If you see the act, pick the puppy up immediately and put it on the papers and praise it when it goes. Gradually remove all but a small patch of papers—the size of the area will depend in part on the size of the puppy. Do not move too fast; two to three weeks is a perfectly acceptable timetable.

If you live in an apartment or where there is no private yard to take your puppy outdoors, you will have to wait until your veterinarian feels that it is safe to expose it to other dogs' germs before you take it out. Otherwise, if you have a private outdoor place where you can take your puppy, you should begin to teach it to relieve itself outdoors at the same time that it is learning to use the papers indoors. Take it out and stay with it, and praise it lavishly when it eliminates outdoors.

Even though you will undoubtedly want your puppy

to eliminate outdoors most of the time, the trick is for it to learn that it is all right to use both places, not simply one or the other. Eventually, you will be providing a permanent papered area inside your house or apartment for your dog to use in emergencies—the "acceptable alternative" that we spoke of above. The old bugaboo about it being confusing for a puppy to use different types of surface is simply not true if you start when your puppy is young. If you wait until a dog is older and set in its ways and then suddenly introduce it to paper (or the outdoors), it may indeed be confused for a while.

As soon as your puppy has some control over its muscles and is ready to concentrate, teach it where you want it to go. During this short period when your puppy is in the process of learning elimination control, you and your family have to pay attention and make an effort to anticipate its needs. If the puppy is out of its room playing with you, for example, and it begins to sniff, circle, and squat on the living room carpet, pick it up immediately and take it either to the papers or outdoors, whichever is closest. Then praise it lavishly when it goes in the right place. If you are not paying attention and the puppy slips up, take it (do not call it) to its infraction and scold it. Do not be overly harsh at this stage, however, and never link punishment to the acceptable area. *Never* rub a puppy's nose in excrement or urine, any more than you would rub a baby's nose in a soiled diaper. Not only is this cruel and offensive, but it serves no useful purpose whatsoever and may make a puppy hide to eliminate! Remember that the puppy is still learning and that excessive punishment will only succeed in causing it to become confused and nervous, which in turn may cause it to eliminate. Patient, consistent, repeated lessons and lavish praise are the best tools to use when housebreaking a puppy. To avoid accidents when you are not able to watch your puppy carefully, confine it to its space where papers are nearby. In fact, confine it at all times when you cannot watch it—even when you are on the telephone.

AN ACCEPTABLE ALTERNATIVE

At the same time that you are teaching your puppy to use the papers and/or the outdoors for elimination, you should also introduce it to what we call an "acceptable alternative." This is a place (papers, or a pan of some sort) where the puppy will learn to go in case it is caught short when you are away from home or are unable to let it out or walk it for some reason.

Choose a spot that is out of the way yet always accessible to the puppy. A basement, cellar, attached garage, or even an upstairs bathroom will do, but it must be within your puppy's enclosure. If you wish to move it later on when your puppy is allowed the run of the house, you can do so gradually if you make sure that the puppy knows where its alternative area is. Remember that your puppy will be *place-trained* to the area, not pan- or paper-trained.

Depending on the size of your puppy, line an appropriate area with newspaper, or paint a low-sided pan or box with several coats of waterproof enamel and line it with paper. For a large dog you may have to rig up or build a painted plywood or metal tray or pan. A discarded metal vegetable display pan from your local supermarket, or an airconditioning drip tray, for instance, may work. Show the puppy where it is and leave it there all of the time. (This is important—otherwise you might forget to put it down when you go out.) If you live in a small apartment, this can be a problem. It is such an important part of your puppy's well-being, however, that it should still be done. In a situation such as this, you can always pick up the paper or pan as soon as you come home and put it down again when you leave. You are not likely to forget it if you are in a small space.

When a male dog is old enough to raise his leg, you have to rig up some kind of upright surface or post for him to use. A fireplace log, stripped of bark and painted,

123

or a simple painted two-by-four piece of lumber, can be nailed from the bottom in the center of the pan. Alternately, you can attach a piece of waterproofed heavy cardboard or plywood to the wall adjacent to the pan. If you use this method, however, be sure that there is not a crack between the pan and the wall area.

This acceptable alternative is rarely used in most households, but it provides valuable insurance and peace of mind for both you and your pet.

SUCCESS?

If you are conscientious and consistent during the early housebreaking period, your puppy should be just about trained to use either the papers in its room, the alternative area, or the outdoors, by the time it is twelve to thirteen weeks old.

Some puppies still have accidents from time to time, especially when they become overexcited. A child who is in sole charge of a puppy after school should be reminded to be sure that the puppy has a chance to go outdoors the minute he walks in the door—not after he has taken off his coat, called a friend on the telephone, or fixed himself a snack. The puppy will be excited by his homecoming and will not be able to wait long before an accident occurs. All family members should learn to watch for signs of squatting in an inappropriate place and should also be reminded to *always* praise a puppy when it eliminates in the right place.

LATER ON

When your puppy has mastered housebreaking and is able to be trusted in other behavior areas, you may want to give it the run of the house when you are out. Even if you don't choose to allow it complete freedom, you may let it have access to some rooms. If you have taught your puppy to use the acceptable alternative in an emergency, you will now be able to remove the newspapers from the floor in its original room and know that it has somewhere to eliminate if necessary in your absence.

WALKING

Even if you have a nice big yard, it is still important for a puppy to be taken on a daily walk as soon as it is properly immunized. Your puppy should get used to walking no matter what the weather. We talk about this in more detail in both *Socialization*, page 108, and in *Leash Walking in Public Places*, page 190.

BACKSLIDING

It is very common for male dogs to seemingly forget everything they ever knew about housebreaking when they become sexually mature and learn to lift their legs to urinate. This usually occurs when a puppy is around eight or nine months old and can be the beginning of sexual marking behavior.

As we discuss in *Castration (Neutering, Altering)*, page 214, this operation usually eliminates marking behavior in male dogs. But until the operation is performed you may have to go back to space confinement for your puppy, especially when you are out and at night, and you will have to vigorously reinforce the housebreaking steps described above. If your puppy lifts his leg excessively when you are walking outdoors, you can discourage this behavior by insisting that the puppy keep walking briskly along and allowing just a few stops to urinate. An uncastrated male may engage in sexual urine marking whenever there is another male dog nearby or a female in heat for miles around, and the male dog usually marks a new house or apartment if you move.

Female dogs engage in sexual urine marking less often than male dogs do, but a female may urine-mark, especially if she is unspayed and there are other dogs in the vicinity when she is in heat. Confinement and reinforcement should remind her that this is not acceptable behavior. It is important to nip this type of behavior in the bud for both males and females.

Severe anxiety can also cause house soiling in a previously well-trained older puppy or adult dog. The sudden absence of a well-loved person or a change in the household makeup may trigger enough anxiety to produce house soiling as can an owner's stress due to illness, death, or any sudden change. You can help prevent this by accustoming your puppy early in life to tolerate the absence of a favorite person (see Chapter 9). In extreme cases, you may find it best to board your pet for a while in order to remove it from a stressful situation.

Sudden loss of control over bowels or bladder should always be cause for concern, although it should not result in house soiling if you have provided a place in your house for your pet to go. If your puppy's elimination habits do change noticeably at any time in its life, consult your veterinarian right away.

If a puppy or dog has been hospitalized or kenneled in a cage for a long period of time, it may seem to "forget" about housebreaking when it returns home. Again, reinforcement and confinement will usually remind your pet of the proper behavior.

Sometime near the end of a puppy's seventh week of life you will probably come to adopt it and take it away from its mother and littermates. If you do not already have another pet at home and you anticipate leaving your puppy alone a great deal, you may want to consider the possibility of adopting more than one puppy (see *Another Pet for Company?* page 250). This can be an excellent way to prevent or lessen behavior problems that can arise due to boredom and loneliness when a puppy is without human companionship for extended periods of time on a regular basis.

Before selecting your new puppy and taking it home, be sure to read Part One of this book.

8

Eight Weeks to Three Months: Learning a Lot

This is a time of great upheaval, change, and learning in your new puppy's life. It is also a period during which you and your puppy begin to know and understand each other.

During this month you lay the groundwork for a trusting, happy, mutually satisfactory relationship with your puppy. You show it what you expect of it in a number of new situations and begin to teach it appropriate behavior. Many of the lessons that you teach your puppy in this first month need to be repeated and reinforced again and again throughout its puppyhood, but if you start right away to work with your puppy's eagerness to please you and its desire to learn, you will have a solid foundation to build on toward raising a satisfactory, well-behaved dog. It is never too early to begin!

You will get to know about your puppy's particular temperament and personality—whether it is strong-willed or compliant, gentle or rambunctious, shy or outgoing, and just what makes it the endearing individual that it is. Whether this is your tenth puppy or your first, these early weeks are a period of discovery and delight for you.

127

Table 16 HIGHLIGHTS CHART *Eight Weeks to Three Months: Learning a Lot*

	PUPPY DEVELOPMENT		OWNER INVOLVEMENT	
	Physical	Social/Behavioral	Puppy's Health/Safety Needs	Working with Puppy Readiness
Eight to Nine Weeks	Permanent teeth begin to erupt	Investigating behavior continues, refined Chewing, biting, mouthing Fearful, cautious	First veterinarian visit Space Management* 4 meals/day† Chew toys (see →) Protect against rough handling (e.g., children)	Routine* Begin to teach Puppy Obedience: Verbal Commands* Correct Inappropriate Chewing, Biting, etc.* Avoid frightening by loud noises and harsh treatment
Nine to Ten Weeks	Motor skills refined Short attention span	Development of dominant/subordinate behavior with other animals‡ Begins to understand/pay attention to owner's wishes Attachment to owner	Gentle grooming begun† Checkup, stool sample; immunizations continued† Protect against exposure to other dogs and dog waste until immunizations are complete or veterinarian gives okay†	Nip Aggression in the Bud* Begin to Accustom to Collar and Leash* Begin to teach Car Manners*

Table 16 HIGHLIGHTS CHART

Eight Weeks to Three Months: Learning a Lot (Cont.)

| | PUPPY DEVELOPMENT | | OWNER INVOLVEMENT | |
	Physical	Social/Behavioral	Puppy's Health/ Safety Needs	Working with Puppy Readiness
Ten to Eleven Weeks		Shows strong dominant/ subordinate behavior with other animals‡		Needs lots of human company/attention Needs "own" time away from other pets, littermates
Eleven Weeks to Three Months	More control over elimination	Comes when called		Begin *serious* Errorless Housebreaking*

* *See Detailed Discussion.*   † See Chapter 4.   ‡ See Chapter 5.

For the puppy, it is both an exciting and a somewhat confusing time. There is a whole new world of special humans and their surroundings to learn about, and all sorts of new experiences to digest. From the very beginning your puppy is anxious to learn how you want it to behave and react, and needs to be shown what is expected of it in its new role as your pet.

The First Week: Starting Off on the Right Foot

It is best to stop off at the veterinarian's office on the way home from the breeder so that your puppy has a thorough checkup. If you have not been able to do so for some reason, you must keep your new puppy isolated from any contact with other household pets until you do.

When you arrive home, carry the puppy to its room (see *Space Management*, page 32) and put it down. Excitement and nervousness may make the puppy thirsty, so be sure that there is fresh water available. You can leave some dry food in a bowl if you wish, but do not try to make the puppy eat right away; its stomach may be upset from the journey home and also from excitement and nerves. The excitement may cause a bout of diarrhea. This is natural and should not be a concern unless it persists for more than twelve hours. Call the veterinarian if you are in doubt.

Give the puppy a pat and speak to it gently, and then leave it alone to explore. As difficult as this may be to do, it is best not to handle the puppy for a while until it has a chance to settle down and investigate its surroundings. It may be exhausted and go to sleep for a while. Let it sleep as long as it wants.

We talk about how to handle the puppy's introduction to a new home and its first night away from its mother and littermates in *Settling In* (page 50), but it bears repeating that its introduction to family members and other pets should be gradual and nonthreatening. Do not scold or discipline a puppy or attempt to teach it any lessons for the first few days. During this time you want your puppy to feel secure, and it has enough new experiences to handle in the early days in your home without the added confusion or worry of being corrected or admonished for reasons that it doesn't yet understand. Gentle play and calm affectionate handling are your best teaching tools for these first days.

An eight-week-old puppy still requires a great deal of sleep every day and should be allowed to rest whenever it seems tired.

You and your family have probably worked out some kind of agreement about care responsibilities, as we suggest in Chapter 2, *Who Will Do What*? Now that the puppy is a reality, it is time to set that agreement into action. For the first day or two, however, an adult or responsible older child should be in charge of overseeing all puppy-care tasks. It is often helpful if each family member does every task at least once as a sort of shake-down so that everyone understands what each job entails in order to make sure that no important details have been overlooked.

This is a good time to discuss the concept of routine as it applies to puppy care.

Routine: How Important Is It?

It is after seven in the evening, and Carol is upset. She has just started a new job and is still in the office. She knows that it will be at least an hour before she gets home and can walk her dog and give him his dinner. She knows that her year-old Boston terrier, Andy, will probably have wet in the house, and will be anxious and starving. Faithful to the instructions to stick to a strict routine that Andy's breeder gave her when she adopted him, she has always walked and fed him by seven at the latest. If this job continues to keep her late most nights (and it looks as if it will), she will have to hire someone to walk and feed her dog every day, which will be expensive.

Beverly used to like to sleep late on Sunday mornings, but she can't anymore. Every day including Sunday, Annie, the golden retriever, begins to whine, then paw, then lick her face, promptly at seven. When she first got Annie as a little puppy Beverly read that it was very important for a dog to become used to a regular routine. So, every morning at seven she took Annie out for a walk and gave her breakfast. She assumed that when Annie grew up, she would be less rigid in her demands, but this hasn't happened. Sighing and dragging herself up, she rues the day that she ever got the dog.

Beverly and Carol have both allowed themselves and their dogs to become slaves to rigid routines. They have created situations that are annoying and nerve-wracking for them. More important, this extreme rigidity creates a potentially anxiety-producing situation for their pets when, inevitably, the routine must be broken.

This is a somewhat controversial area in puppy rearing. Many breeders and veterinarians, possibly fearful of a hit-or-miss attitude on owner's parts, recommend rigid routines when it comes to feeding, exercising, and other puppy-care tasks. They reason that it is easier for an owner to remember to perform care activities if they are regularly scheduled and that a puppy should know when to expect to eat, go out, and so forth. A new puppy owner can be so intimidated by the need for a rigid schedule that she turns her life upside down in order to comply.

We believe that, although *consistency* (in the sense of cause and effect both in regard to routines and to actions and reactions) is extremely important in raising a puppy, *rigidity* should be avoided. It certainly is true

132

that very young puppies must be fed and tended to on a regular basis, but by the time a puppy is eight or nine weeks old, some flexibility can be built into any schedule. Commonsense flexibility such as varying mealtime by ten or fifteen minutes to begin with does not equate with carelessness or neglect.

As a puppy gets older it should expect to be walked and fed when its owner gets up or comes home whatever time that may be within reason. Certainly, if an owner occasionally expects to get home very late, it is a good idea for someone to feed a dog, but a delay of an hour or so should not send either owner or dog into a panic. This, by the way, is another advantage of our Errorless Housebreaking, which appeared in the previous chapter.

If they had not brought their puppies up to expect everything to occur on a rigid schedule, Carol would have been able to relax and finish her work, and Beverly could have continued to get a few hours of extra sleep on Sundays. Andy and Annie, respectively, would have waited patiently for dinner and breakfast until their owners were ready to give it to them, and neither the dogs nor their owners would have been anxious and upset by slight variations in their usual routines.

In the beginning you should feed your puppy the kind of food it has been used to eating. It should be given four meals a day unless you are using the ad-lib feeding method. Feeding times should be relaxed and calm, and a puppy should never be exercised or played with roughly immediately after eating, or it will probably throw up. A puppy will probably take a nap immediately after eating and eliminating. In Chapter 4 we discuss all aspects of feeding, amounts and types of food, and so forth.

By the end of the first week, your puppy should feel completely at home and be ready to concentrate and learn more about what you expect of it.

Good Habits Begin Early

As soon as your puppy gets over its initial confusion, it is time to begin to teach it a few simple lessons. Some puppies are ready in a couple of days, while it takes others a bit longer. You will know when your puppy is ready to learn by its reactions. If it immediately bounces over to you or a family member when you enter its space and follows you around eagerly as you do your chores, it is more than ready to begin to learn a few simple verbal commands.

Puppy Obedience: Verbal Commands

The doorbell rang just as Richard was about to leave for work. While he held the door ajar in order to sign for a package, a group of children went by on the street. Tammy, a four-year-old Cairn terrier, loved children, and before Richard could react, she had darted out the door and down the street after them. Rushing out to the curb, Richard called loudly. Tammy glanced over her shoulder at him and continued down the sidewalk. Worried that she might go into the street and be hit by a car, Richard began to run after her, calling continuously. Seeing him, she began to run faster. Fortunately, one of the children saw what was happening and was able to grab Tammy. As Richard panted toward home carrying the dog, he wondered why she hadn't come when he called her.

It is important to start to teach your puppy its name and some basic verbal commands right away for its own safety and to lay the groundwork for later obedience learning. Your young puppy is very anxious to please you and eager to gain your approval. At this stage, your puppy is very dependent on you. You are the center of your puppy's world, and it is not difficult to get it to pay attention to you. When your puppy is a little older, it will

134

be a lot more independent and usually a lot harder to teach.

Initially you will teach your puppy at home. Because a puppy's attention span is very short when it is young, you have to keep your lessons short. Five minutes is probably the maximum time you should spend for each session in the very beginning. As the puppy grows you can spend more time according to its ability to concentrate. If possible, give two or three lessons a day, every day. Never hold the lessons when a puppy is hungry, but if you try to teach it immediately after a meal, it will probably go right to sleep. It is best to work alone with a puppy in the beginning so that it isn't distracted, and your first lessons should be very relaxed and informal. You want to retain your puppy's trust, so never be harsh or cross with it. The trick is to work with its desire to please you and to show it patiently and calmly what it is you want it to do.

Later on, when your puppy has been completely immunized and it is safe to expose it to other dogs, we strongly recommend puppy obedience school.

LEARNING ITS NAME

As soon as you can, decide what you are going to call your puppy and begin speaking to it by name. It is usually easier for a puppy to learn (and for you to use) a one-syllable word than a big mouthful, so even if you decide to name it Mr. Bojangles or Lady Victoria, you will probably want to call your puppy Bo or Vicky.

Your puppy will quickly learn to come running whenever anyone comes into its room, and every family member should learn to address it by name as often as possible: "Hi, Bo," "Good girl, Vicky," and so forth. Speak to it often, whatever you and your puppy are doing, and always use its name. Practice calling its name when it is across the room from you, and praise it when it comes. Within a week your puppy should know its name.

COME

As soon as your puppy knows its name, you can begin to teach it a few simple verbal commands. If you sit on the floor, your puppy almost always will come running to you. Use this natural action to teach it to "come" on command. Sit down, clap your hands to get its attention, and say, "Come, Bo," and the puppy will come running. Praise him lavishly. You can also give a food treat at this stage in the training, but be sure to give praise also so that you can eliminate the food treat later on. It doesn't matter that Bo would have come to you anyway, without the command. You are teaching him to listen to you and react even if he doesn't yet realize it.

Get up and move around the room and call your puppy. Sometimes, if the puppy is chewing on a toy or playing with another person, you may have to clap your hands to capture its attention. Clap and call, using the puppy's name. If it responds immediately, it should be praised. If the puppy does not respond right away, go and get it and bring it over to the spot you were in. You can offer a treat if necessary in order to lure the puppy to you, or you can tug gently on a leash attached to a collar. But do not give up at this stage or the puppy will learn an early lesson that it can ignore you whenever it wants to. Always follow through and enforce your command in one way or another so that the puppy does not get the idea that it is all right to play a "catch me if you can" game, as Tammy did in the anecdote above.

NO!

This extremely important verbal command cannot be taught, of course, in lessons. You must wait until the puppy does something you do not want it to do. A firm tone of voice is essential in order to convey your displeasure when you say "No!" and you can add whatever other words or word you like, such as "No bite," "No jump," and so on as long as the 'No" part is strong and easily identifiable by the puppy. Never yell or shout, however, or you will frighten and confuse the puppy. You may have to begin by clapping your hands sharply at the same time that you say 'No" in order to capture your puppy's attention. If the puppy stops what it is doing and comes running to you, praise it. But if it goes right back to the unwanted action, you have to say "No" again and perhaps take steps to stop the behavior. As we discuss in various other places, you can also give the puppy an acceptable alternative—a chew stick, for instance, instead of the corner of the rug. Be very careful, however, that the puppy does not associate your verbal "No" with the acceptable alternative, or it will be very confused. Say "No," and if the puppy stops the unwanted action and runs to you, then play with it briefly and give it the alternative.

OTHER VERBAL COMMANDS

Once your puppy has learned to come when you call it by name, it is ready to learn a few more verbal commands. After the puppy has run to you and been praised, it will probably stand wagging its tail looking up at you as if to ask "Now, what?" Instead of immediately initiating a game or whatever, put your hand on the puppy's back and rub along the spine from the head to the tail, around the tail to the hind legs, and push gently on the joint of the hind legs, while you say "Sit." The pressure of your hand will probably cause the puppy to sit down, at which point you should praise it lavishly. Another successful method is to hold a small food treat between your thumb and finger and, beginning just under the puppy's chin, slowly raise your hand up above its nose while you say "Sit." As the puppy follows your hand with its eyes, its head will go up and back, and it will usually sit down. When it does, give it the treat and a lot of praise. After a few lessons, try simply saying "Sit" without touching the puppy or offering a treat. If the puppy has gotten the idea, tell it that it is the smartest puppy in the world. If not, repeat the lesson a few more times.

To teach a puppy to lie down, face in the same direction as the puppy and kneel beside it on its right side. With your left arm, reach over the puppy's back and grasp its left paw. At the same time, grasp its right paw with your right hand. Lift both paws gently forward as you say "Down," and the puppy will be lying down. This should be performed in a very relaxed manner without pulling. Praise it enthusiastically. Again, it should get the idea in just a few lessons.

If you leave a puppy lying down for more than a few minutes, it will probably drift off to sleep. This is the ultimate time to teach the "Down, stay" command. Get a book or magazine and sit beside the puppy while it sleeps for a half hour. If the puppy wakes up before thirty minutes have elapsed, say "Down, stay," and put it back down if necessary. After the half hour, get up, and the puppy will probably wake; then you can praise it lavishly again.

PUPPY OBEDIENCE CLASSES

Puppy obedience classes have become very popular and can be found in many communities. Your veterinarian, local ASPCA or humane society, a dog breeder, or other puppy owners may be able to help you locate a puppy school.

We strongly recommend that you take your puppy to obedience school as soon as it is old enough to associate with other dogs. It is important for a puppy to learn to listen to you and obey you even when there are other dogs and other people around to distract it.

If you are not an experienced dog handler, obedience school is very useful for you, too. It will show you how to teach your puppy effectively. Even though your puppy wants to please you, it cannot do so unless you know how to show it what you want in a clear, uncomplicated manner.

As we mention in *Nip Aggression in the Bud* (page 146) in this chapter, obedience school can also be a very useful experience for a youngster, especially one who tends to be aggressive. The child will learn how to control a puppy without resorting to anger or violent actions.

If you have an opportunity, visit a session of the puppy obedience class before enrolling and observe the instructor. Unfortunately, there are still a few dog trainers who are much too harsh and punitive and will only succeed in terrorizing a puppy. You know your own puppy best and can judge its response to training methods. If the trainer is too harsh, don't enroll in that class. If you have already enrolled, drop out and request a refund. You do not want your puppy's natural desire to please and its good nature spoiled by harsh treatment. If you cannot find another class, you should teach your puppy at home.

Take It Easy

Even though your puppy may seem pretty grown up in a number of ways, it is still lacking in judgment. When family members take a puppy out of its room into the rest of the house or out to an enclosed yard, they must remember that it has to be watched all the time. If there are young children in the family, it is a good rule to permit them to take the puppy from its room only when an adult or responsible older youngster is present. It is too easy for young children to become distracted and forget to watch a puppy. Even the clumsiest-seeming puppy can move amazingly fast at times, and it doesn't take more than a minute for a puppy to wander into the street, chew on an electric cord, or fall down a stairwell.

All puppies go through what has been called a fear period sometime around eight or nine weeks of age. It seems to be a time of intense awareness of the sights and sounds of the environment, and the fearfulness is more pronounced in some puppies. If you notice that your puppy suddenly seems afraid of new objects and people, and cringes, backs off, or starts at loud noises or sudden motions, take it easy for a while and don't push the puppy into new experiences. Don't allow a fearful puppy to become traumatized by rough handling, loud noises, or harsh treatment during this time. Potentially frightening events such as first-time nail clipping or professional grooming should be put off for a week or two until this stage is outgrown. Children should be reminded that the puppy is still a baby and that there will be plenty of time for roughhousing later on when it gets bigger and more used to them.

This does not mean that training has to go by the wayside, however. Gentle, patient training is not frightening and is always the best way to prevent potentially annoying habits. One of the first natural actions that your eight- or nine-week-old puppy immediately begins to indulge in is chewing. At this stage, the puppy's adult teeth are erupting, and the urge to chew and bite is overwhelming.

Inappropriate Chewing, Mouthing, Biting, and Pica

Six-year-old Jimmy and his friend are quietly playing an elaborate game on the floor using plastic dinosaur and caveman models. Suddenly Jimmy's mother hears a shriek. Running out of the kitchen, she sees Jimmy racing up the stairs after Sheba, their nine-month-old Sheltie puppy. "She took the tyrannosaurus," he screams as he tries to grab Sheba. Mother joins the chase, but by the time they reach the dog under the bed, the dinosaur's tail has been chewed off. Jimmy is in tears and vows that he "hates that stupid dog. She always ruins everything." Mother is also understandably upset; the afternoon's quiet has been permanently shattered, and this scene has been repeated too many times to be easily dismissed. She suspects that Sheba thinks of it as a game, and she does not know how to handle it.

This scene is only one example of the kinds of inappropriate chewing, mouthing, and biting puppies often indulge in. Pica, or the eating of unnatural, inedible things, is another form of inappropriate chewing behavior that some puppies develop.

If you watch puppies playing with each other, you will notice that they do a great deal of mouthing and chewing and often nip each other in a seemingly friendly manner. Because chewing and mouthing are such natural behaviors for puppies, and because your puppy teethes almost continuously for seven months after you get it, it is very important to teach a puppy right away what is and what is not appropriate to chew.

NIPPING (BITING) AND MOUTHING PEOPLE

When you first bring your puppy home, its mouth will probably be everywhere. It tries to bite fingers, toes, noses, ankles, and heels. Don't let the puppy get away with this, and don't allow other family members to permit this either. Even though it may seem "cute" at first, nipping soon begins to be annoying. The dog does not "outgrow" this habit on its own, and it becomes worse and hurts more as the puppy grows. As soon as your very young puppy begins to nip, grab its snout in one hand, say "No" or "No chew" or whatever. *Or* stop it immediately and put something appropriate that it *can* chew in its mouth. Do not make the mistake of saying "No" at the same time that you give the puppy something appropriate to chew, or you will be conveying a contradictory message. Either stop it, grab its muzzle, and say "No," or stop it and give it an appropriate chew toy. Small, long chew sticks made of rawhide are excellent, but *only when you are around*, because a puppy can choke on small pieces that might break off. More important, if a puppy runs with a long chew stick in its mouth, the stick can spear the dog's throat and kill it, just as a lollipop stick can kill a small child.

As the puppy gets bigger, knotted chew bones should be substituted. They are safer for a puppy when it is alone since they cannot spear a dog's throat. Although they are meant to be digestible, some puppies with very strong jaws and teeth can break off too many pieces and swallow them. Usually these pieces are digested or vomited, but there have been instances of hunks of rawhide becoming impacted in a puppy's digestive tract. So take care and observe your puppy, and if it seems to eat many pieces of rawhide, give it a chew toy with larger knots that is harder to break chunks from, or give the toy only when you are around. A puppy should always have something digestible to chew. As it gets older and its teeth become less sharp, a nylon bone can be substituted.

If you are consistent and always stop a puppy from biting or nipping you and others, by stopping it and either scolding it or substituting an appropriate chew toy, you should have no trouble teaching your puppy not to nip humans.

Sometimes a dog begins again to "mouth" people when it is older, and in doing so may also nip or bite. At this time in a dog's life, these actions appear to be signs of affection and may even be somewhat sexual in origin. Some owners call this "love nipping" and may tolerate it. It really should not be allowed, however, because it can hurt, especially if the dog is large, and your friends may not understand or enjoy it at all. Stop the dog immediately. Grasp its muzzle and say "NO." At the same time make it clear that you have withdrawn your attention and approval for the moment by breaking off whatever activity you were engaged in with the puppy. You can begin to interact again with the puppy in a few minutes, but if it starts to nip again, repeat your scolding and withdrawal.

CHEWING OBJECTS

Some dogs develop the habit of chewing on household objects or people's clothing. Others, like Sheba in the anecdote above, attack and grab an object that someone is playing with or using and then run away, making a "game" of it.

A puppy that chews on things when it is left alone may be exhibiting signs of Boredom and Destructive Behavior, which we discuss in Chapter 14, or may simply be going through a bad siege of teething. Whatever the cause, this habit should be broken as quickly as possible, before it becomes ingrained. Not only can it be dangerous for the puppy and destructive for your household, but it can also be a serious fire hazard if wires are chewed, for example. If a puppy begins to chew on something inappropriate (that is, anything except its own chew toy) while you are around, the steps described above to deter nipping humans can be followed: Stop the pup immediately, hold its muzzle, and scold it. Better yet, remove the puppy from the area and then give it an appropriate chew toy. Do not give the puppy a chew toy when it is still in the vicinity of the not-to-be-chewed object because we have found that puppies often go from one object to another when they are chewing.

If the puppy chews only when you are not there, the first and most obvious step is to remove from reach, if possible, whatever it is the puppy is chewing on and substitute a desirable chew toy that is reserved only for your absences. As we also suggest in *Boredom and Destructive Behavior*, it always helps to tire a puppy out with exercise or play before you leave. If these measures are not effective, you may have to treat whatever object or objects the puppy is apt to chew with a vile-tasting deterrent. Bitter Apple works for small, sensitive dogs, but larger breeds may require something stronger. Some kind of quinine-based solution is usu-

143

ally effective, such as Thumb (used to stop children from sucking their thumbs) and No Chew (available in most pet-supply stores). If none of these deterrents works, experiment in your spice and food cabinets to find something edible that repels your dog. We have found that the most effective punishment is one the animal brings on itself—in this case by biting or chewing a horrid-tasting thing. When you return home and find that your puppy has *not* chewed anything inappropriate, heap it with lavish praise.

In the case of a snatch-and-run attention-getting chewer like Sheba it is important not to let the dog think that it has invented a wonderful new game. Jimmy should be told not to race after Sheba because this is just what she wants. Instead, Mother should immediately go upstairs, get Sheba, take away the toy, and severely scold her verbally. If this is not effective, the next step is to set up a situation in which a plastic toy is saturated with strong repellent and put in Sheba's path so that she will grab it. The children should be in on the ruse, but do not use this method with a very young child who might put the toy in his own mouth.

PICA

Pica, the actual ingestion of inedible things such as earth, stones, or bits of cloth; and coprophagia, the eating of feces, are much harder to deter, and the causes are often very hard to determine. They can sometimes be attributed to severe stress and boredom, and possibly there is an underlying physical reason for this behavior—a dietary deficiency that the puppy is trying to correct, for instance. Whatever the reason, severe or continued pica can lead to serious physical problems— intestinal blockage for example, or ruined teeth if a puppy chews on stones. Coprophagia is less physically dangerous but is certainly unpleasant and usually results in a severe infestation of intestinal parasites.

The first step in treating these disturbances is a thorough physical examination of the puppy by a veterinarian to attempt to find out if there is a physical cause. Sometimes dietary supplementation helps but this should be undertaken only under a veterinarian's supervision.

If no underlying physical cause is determined, these habits have to be treated as behavioral in nature. The best method for deterring a puppy from eating inedible things is a set-up situation such as we described above. In cases of both pica and coprophagia, normal repellents are usually not effective and extra-strong-tasting substances must be used.

As your puppy gets older and becomes stronger in the next weeks, it requires less sleep and begins to explore even more. You may be surprised at the seemingly overnight refinement of your puppy's motor skills and its ability to go places and do things that it could not accomplish merely days ago. Examine your puppy's quarters with a new viewpoint and be sure that it cannot reach objects you don't want it to, climb on furniture that it couldn't before or escape from its room.

If you haven't begun to accustom your puppy to gentle grooming, now is the time to do so. Most puppies enjoy the process of being handled and combed or brushed, and the sooner they become accustomed to regular grooming and overall inspection, the better. A grooming session is excellent for you to spend time quietly with your puppy, talking to it, and it provides a good opportunity to strengthen the bond between you. Grooming is described in more detail in Chapter 4.

Sometime around nine or ten weeks of age, your puppy may begin to demonstrate dominant behavior toward a human member of the family or toward another pet. It may even decide to challenge your authority. This is the time to "nip aggression in the bud." (See also *Inter-Dog Aggression*, page 166).

Nip Aggression in the Bud

Joe is a strapping twelve-year-old who likes to play contact sports. From the time that the family got their boxer, Rex, Joe has been playing tug-of-war with the dog. Both of them seem to love the game, and the boy always rewards Rex with lots of petting and romping after a good "tug." Although Joe's mother has been concerned to hear Rex growl in play from time to time, Joe and his father say that this is perfectly all right, that it is "natural" and part of "getting into the game." Yesterday, Rex bit Joe badly on the hand when the boy tried to take the pull-toy out of his mouth.

Two-year-old Robbie toddles up to Lucky, the family's Westie, and watches as the dog chews on a bone. Sitting on the ground next to the dog, Robbie begins to pet her on the head. Lucky growls and moves away, taking the bone with her. Robbie follows her and begins to pet her again. Suddenly, Lucky growls again and nips the baby on the nose. Robbie's mother rushes in when the child howls, grabs him up, and shouts "Bad dog" at Lucky, kicking at her. Lucky backs off, growling more loudly. Obviously, the dog must go.

These are two examples of aggressive behavior that could have been easily avoided. In the first instance, Rex's naturally aggressive instincts were constantly encouraged in fiercely competitive play. In the second, Lucky had obviously not been taught that an appropriate human has the right to approach her no matter what she's doing, and even to take things from her; she had never learned not to be overterritorial or protective of "her" things.

DOMINANCE-GENTLING: HOW TO TEACH A PUPPY NOT TO BE AGGRESSIVE

It is never too early to teach a puppy that aggressive behavior toward humans is not acceptable. Some dogs are naturally more aggressive or dominant than others,

146

and they must learn right away that they cannot get away with it. It is never "all right" for a dog to protect its property or food from a person unless that person is a criminal who is trespassing or attacking the dog's home or family.

The biggest mistake an owner can make is to allow a puppy to get away with an aggressive act. No matter how small a puppy is, if it growls, grabs an object and runs away from you, or tries to nip aggressively, *act immediately.*

You should react the same way you would if a child threw a tantrum. Get down on the floor and use both hands to hold the puppy down firmly while you remain kneeling above it. Be sure the puppy's head is facing away from you, and keep your own face away from the puppy's or you could be bitten. You can reinforce your actions with a verbal 'No" or "Stop that," but the important thing is to hold the puppy down quietly while speaking firmly until it stops growling and struggling and is calm and relaxed. Then you can release the puppy and immediately repeat whatever action it was that triggered its aggressive reaction in the first place. If the puppy acts aggressively again, repeat the restraint again until the message is clear. We call this kind of treatment "dominance-gentling." In effect, you are letting the puppy know that you are dominant to it. A word of *warning* must be said here: Make it very clear to any youngsters in your household that they must *not* attempt this procedure. This is an action that should be taken only by an adult or responsible older child. If a young child attempts it, he may get badly bitten. What is more, a too-rough child could hurt a puppy and/or misuse the procedure.

Never react to a puppy's aggressiveness by hitting. This will only excite the puppy further and may prompt an even stronger aggressive reaction on its part. This is especially true if you are dealing with a dog that has an inherently aggressive nature to begin with, such as a terrier.

These dominance-gentling actions should be repeated every time a puppy acts aggressively toward any human, not just you. Children should be taught, of course, not to take food away from a dog, but if a toddler or young child should do so, the dog should allow it. A dog should not consider it all right to protect anything, not even a food dish, by acting aggressively toward family members or friends.

AVOID ENCOURAGING TERRITORIALLY ORIENTED AGGRESSIVE BEHAVIOR

As we discuss in *Space Management*, (page 32), a puppy should never be brought up to think of any area or any object as belonging to it. It is unfortunately very easy to encourage this kind of territorial behavior by providing a puppy with a stationary bed or crate or whatever to sleep in and by allowing the animal to feel that it can then protect "its" space from other pets and people. In the same way, toys and objects can soon become "possessions" that the puppy feels it must guard with aggressive actions. You would not put up with this type of behavior in a child and should not allow it to develop in a puppy. Imagine if your son growled at you or bit you when you went into his room or sat on "his" chair!

It is especially important to avoid encouragement of this type of territorial behavior with breeds of dogs that are often territorial by nature (terriers, for example). The problem can be easily compounded when humans back away at the first sign of a growl or other protective behavior on the part of the dog. This is one reason we recommend that a dog's bed be portable and that toys, bones, and feeding dishes be interchangeable and constantly handled and picked up by people. At the first sign that a puppy thinks that it can protect "its" property either by growling, nipping, or running away with an object and hiding, you should immediately react as we described above and should continuously handle and move any objects that the puppy treats overprotectively.

AVOID ENCOURAGING AGGRESSION THROUGH "PLAY"

The first example given above is actually another form of what we call "Negative Reinforcement" (see Chapter 15). In this case, Joe and his parents have encouraged Rex to engage in aggressive behavior. By playing an intrinsically aggressive game with the dog and egging him on toward more and more overt aggression, Joe was not only tolerating but encouraging Rex's competitive actions—vying with and growling at a human. This is a potentially dangerous game to play with any dog but most particularly with a puppy that demonstrates an aggressive bent from the beginning. It should come as no surprise when a dog, allowed to be aggressive and competitive in daily "play" and encouraged in this response, cannot make the sudden transition away from this behavior but acts in a competitive, aggressive manner when the "game" is over.

There are many other active, rough-and-tumble games that energetic boys can play with equally energetic puppies that do not encourage or abet aggression. Toss and fetch is an especially good game to teach a potentially competitive dog. Both puppy and boy can get lots of exercise, and the puppy learns early on that giving up its prize (stick, ball, and so forth) is the only way to prolong the game.

One thing that parents of an aggressive child must be careful of is that the child does not transfer this trait to a puppy. If they recognize that a child is aggressive or potentially aggressive, they must monitor the child's interaction with a puppy and channel it into nonaggressive play. It can be very helpful to take an aggressive child to obedience class with you and your puppy and if possible allow the child to be the trainer who then teaches other family members obedience commands and routines. This teaches the child how to use appro-

149

priate methods of control over the puppy instead of re-sorting to anger and aggressive actions to control the puppy when it does not do what the child wants it to.

If a puppy does exhibit aggression in play—for ex-ample, refusing to give up a toy or growling when asked to do so—immediate action (see above) should be taken. An adult must be the one who engages in the dominance-gentling of a puppy for the reasons we stated above and because, again, if an overly aggres-sive or angry child is allowed to undertake this task, he may be too harsh, resulting in the dog's learning a neg-ative lesson. An aggressive adult can also have the same negative effect on a puppy, of course, but this may be harder to recognize and/or control.

AVOID AGGRESSION BY NOT ADOPTING YOUR PUPPY TOO YOUNG

In the section on socialization in this chapter, we talk about the fact that there are a number of reasons why it is not a good idea to take a puppy away from the litter before it is at least seven, and preferably eight, weeks of age. It should be reiterated here that if a puppy is not allowed to go through the final two weeks of social-ization within the litter, it misses out on important les-sons of social interaction and often develops into an aggressive puppy.

As the puppies in a litter become bigger and stronger during their last two weeks together, they engage in vigorous play and play-fighting with one another. A puppy learns just how far it can go in these play-fights with its siblings, and that if it is overly aggressive or hurts a littermate, it will suffer retaliation. When a puppy is removed from the interaction of the litter too young, it is deprived of this important lesson, and its adoptive owners have to assume the role of its sisters and broth-ers. The puppy then practices aggression on them, and they have to teach it not to be aggressive.

Premature adoption of a puppy is one cause of ag-

gression that is extremely easy to avoid if you are aware
of it.

The Great Big World

Depending on your own veterinarian's schedule and on
when your puppy's breeder began its immunization series,
your puppy requires a visit to the veterinarian for vaccination sometime during this month. If it has not been performed before, your veterinarian will undoubtedly want to
examine a stool sample for worms.

As we stress in Chapter 4, it is very important to protect
your puppy against exposure to other dogs and their wastes
until it is completely immunized against contagious diseases, or until your veterinarian deems that it is safe from
possible contagion. In most instances this means that your
puppy should not be walked anywhere other dogs might
have frequented.

It is not too early, however, to get your puppy ready for
trips abroad.

Accustom Your Puppy to Wearing a Collar
and Leash

An image comes to mind of the frequently seen paint-
ing of a puppy sitting braced on the ground, pulling
frantically backward against a collar and leash. This
balking puppy was probably not introduced to a collar
and leash until the day it was taken outdoors for a walk
and had its picture painted. It was alarmed at the sudden restraint around its neck and did not know what
was expected of it, so it simply sat down and refused
to budge—a perfectly normal reaction. In the meantime,
whoever is at the other end of the leash is pulling frantically, and the whole event has turned into a tug-of-war
and battle of wills. This need not happen if you accustom your puppy to wearing a collar gradually and then

151

get it used to walking along with you on a leash in the calm and safety of its own home and yard. Then, when it is time to graduate to walking in a public place, the experience will not be frightening or strange for the puppy because it will know how to react. See also *Leash Walking in Public Places*, page 190.

Your puppy should become used to the feel of a collar around its neck as early as possible. As soon as the puppy is settled into your household, measure its neck with a cloth tape measure or piece of soft string held loosely around the neck behind the ears. Use this measurement as a guide and purchase a collar that is the next largest in size—most collars are sized at about two-inch intervals. You will want one that is a bit large to accommodate a puppy's rapid growth. A collar should never be taut on a puppy's neck but should have slack of at least one and half inches, or the width of two sideways-held fingers. Bear in mind that you will probably have to buy at least four or more different collars as the puppy's neck gets larger, so don't buy the most expensive variety.

A collar for a puppy should be soft and light. Metal collars are not desirable for any dog, no matter how large. They are heavy, hard, uncomfortable, and can pinch skin and pull hairs. The nylon "choke" collars in various widths that are now on the market are suitable for all dogs. We put the word "choke" in quotation marks because it has such an unfortunate connotation, especially for uninformed people. A choke collar is not intended to be cruel, punitive, or excessively tight. For those who do not know, it is a collar in which one end slides through a ring; the leash is then attached to this running end. When a puppy is relaxed and not pulling on the leash, the collar remains slack. When a puppy pulls on the leash, the collar tightens and presses on the dog's neck. As soon as the animal stops pulling, the collar loosens again and the pressure stops. A choke collar is a useful tool when you are teaching a puppy how to walk on a leash properly. It is especially useful, and even necessary, if you have a large, strong, or hyperactive puppy who may otherwise pull you excessively. In effect, the puppy itself has control over the collar's pressure. This is another example of a punishment being effective because it is one a puppy brings on itself and will quickly learn how to avoid.

GETTING USED TO WEARING A COLLAR

Put the collar on the puppy. Some puppies do not even notice that they have a collar on, but most shake their heads, run around, and possibly try to paw the collar off. Leave the collar on for only a few minutes and do not let the puppy become overexcited. Pet the puppy and praise it while the collar is on, then take the collar off.

Repeat this procedure several times a day until the puppy accepts the collar calmly. Then you can let it stay on for longer periods of time, but always be sure to remove it when you leave the puppy. Puppies can easily get a collar caught on something in your absence and hurt themselves or even choke themselves to death trying to get free. Designate a particular place, such as a hook in the hallway, kitchen, or puppy's room, where the collar and leash are always kept and include a reminder in your "security" checklist (see Table 8, Chapter 2) to be sure that the collar is off the puppy and in its place each time the puppy is left alone.

GETTING USED TO WALKING ON A LEASH

Although your puppy cannot be taken out in public until it has had all of its immunizations and is pronounced ready by the veterinarian, it can be accustomed to leash walking so that it is prepared when the time comes to go out in the world. When you purchase the first collar, get a leash at the same time. A leash can be a one-time purchase and does not have to be changed as the puppy grows, so you can afford to get a good one. Spring-retractable leashes are extremely useful, especially if you live in the country or suburbs where you may want to allow your puppy to wander and sniff a bit at times. They come in several different strengths and lengths for varying weights and sizes of dogs. Although they are expensive, they are lightweight and won't drag a puppy down, and you can buy one that will be suitable for your dog when it is grown. If you prefer a more traditional leash, lightweight woven nylon leads are very sturdy and last quite a long time.

Practice in the house at first and then in your yard if you have one. Clip the leash on the running end of the collar and walk away from the puppy. When you have gone several feet, call the puppy. (In the meantime, you will be teaching it to respond to its name, as discussed in *Learning Its Name,* page 135. As the puppy comes to you, continue to walk away slowly, and the puppy will probably follow. That, by the way, is another advantage of teaching a puppy to walk on a leash early in its life: Most puppies follow people around eagerly when they are small. If it does not follow or bolts off in another direction, the collar tightens and the puppy has to stop. Stand still and call the puppy. Do not ever pull on the leash or drag the puppy. Let it learn that it can control the collar's pressure by itself, by coming to you and walking with you. As the puppy approaches you, the collar loosens up. As soon as it does, walk away again and encourage the puppy to follow you. When the puppy begins to get the idea, give it lavish praise. Never allow a puppy to chew on its leash.

During this time your puppy becomes increasingly attached to you and your family. It follows you around and wants to be with you all of its waking hours. This is an excellent opportunity to begin to teach it to ride in the car with you. If you have more than one pet, and especially if you have two puppies from the same litter (see *Another Pet for Company?* page 250), each puppy needs to spend some time alone with you or with members of your family, without the other animal. This is very important if the puppy is going to grow into an independent individual with its own relationships, responses, and attachments to people. A car ride is an excellent way to spend time alone with a puppy, while at the same time you introduce it to the larger world around it without exposing it to disease. Frequent, short car rides can be a pleasurable experience for both of you as long as your puppy learns how to behave in a car early in life.

Car Manners

Although she had made the veterinarian's appointment late in the afternoon so that the school children wouldn't be walking home while they were on their way to his office, Liz was still very nervous about taking Buddy, her three-year-old German shepherd, in the car. The last time had been awful. Just as she turned their corner, a group of young boys ran past the car on the way home. Buddy had become very excited and jumped from the backseat into the front seat and onto her lap, causing her to lose control of the car. Luckily, all she had hit was a ditch and no damage had been done to the car, but she had been badly shaken. This time she was armed with a box of dog biscuits to toss back to Buddy one at a time as a distraction in case something or someone exciting appeared. She just wished that she had someone else to ride in the car with them and keep the dog quiet.

A puppy should begin to learn proper car manners the first time that it rides with you to visit the veterinarian. However, if a puppy goes in the car only to visit the veterinarian or the groomer, it may associate automobile trips with potentially stressful situations and react nervously every time it gets in a car. Your puppy can take car rides with you even before it is safe for it to venture into public places, and the more often it is allowed to accompany you on simple "joy rides," the

more apt it is to enjoy and anticipate car rides with pleasure and to learn how to behave in the car.

Some puppies get car sick when they are young. This
can be due to nerves and uneasiness, but it also can
be the result of genuine motion sickness. Usually, a
puppy outgrows this tendency as soon as it becomes
accustomed to riding in a car, but if it becomes a real
problem, your veterinarian may prescribe something to
help allay it. It also helps to have short practice trips,
frequent stops for air and walking, and to take care not
to allow a puppy to eat or drink for at least two hours
before a car trip.

TEACHING CAR MANNERS

Decide ahead of time where you want your puppy to
ride. Your decision should be based on several things:
how large your puppy will eventually grow, how easily
you are distracted when you drive, and whether or not
you usually will be alone in the car with your puppy or
have a human passenger riding in the front seat.

Many dog breeders and owners advocate always having a dog travel in a crate or carrying case in the car
for the dog's safety. A crate or cage for a large dog may
make sense if you have a large station wagon or van,
but it is hardly practical if you have a two-door compact
car. In addition, in order for a crate or cage to afford
real protection for a dog in case of an accident, it would
have to be too small for the dog to stretch out or move
around comfortably. The same is true of a carrying case
for a small dog; it may be useful on short trips but does
not allow the animal enough space if you're on the road
for more than an hour.

In general, we advocate having your puppy learn to
sit or lie quietly on the backseat or on the front seat
beside you. The puppy's collar and leash should be right
by you but not on the puppy, especially if the puppy
rides in the back of the car or will be left in the car at
all. It is far too easy for a puppy to catch a collar on a
door handle or gear shift and choke itself. If, however,

your puppy rides next to you on the front seat and gets out of the car as soon as you stop, you may want to leave its collar on so that you can grasp it if necessary in the process of teaching the puppy to sit or lie still.

Your puppy should have learned the basic instruction, "Sit," right away (see *Puppy Obedience: Verbal Commands*, page 134). It should learn to jump into the car by itself as early as possible, but you may have to pick it up and put it in the car at first. Place it wherever you want it to be and tell it to sit. Pat the puppy and tell it that it's good. Start the car and keep watching the puppy as you drive. It is all right to allow it to stand up and look out of a closed window, or lie down and go to sleep, but don't let it walk around too much; it may wander into your lap or, if it's in the back, jump over the back of the seat. If it starts to do either of these things, pull over to the side of the road, stop the car, firmly put it back where you want it to be, and tell it to sit quietly. While it is behaving well you can praise it, but be careful not to be too verbally enthusiastic or it may mistakenly think it's all right to come to you for a pat or a hug. Make it clear to the puppy that it should not move when you stop until you put its collar and leash on and say it is time to get out. Also practice telling your puppy to stay while you get out and leave it alone in the car for a few minutes.

As soon as your puppy seems to have the idea of sitting or lying quietly while the car is in motion and when you stop for a light or at an intersection, make a point of driving where you know there is activity—children or other dogs on or near the street. This is the acid test of how well your puppy has learned its early lessons. If it reacts to these outside stimuli by jumping around in the car, barking, or otherwise acting wild, pull over, stop the car, and insist that it return to its place and stay quietly. Once it has calmed down, resume your drive, but stop again if the puppy becomes overexcited. As your puppy gets older and goes out on a leash with you, the socialization to people and other animals you give it will help it to know how to act all the time, even when it is in the car.

A COUPLE OF "DON'TS"

All dogs seem to enjoy riding with their heads sticking out of car windows. Don't let your puppy do this. It is really very dangerous. A dog can easily fall or be bumped out of an open window onto the road. More frequently, its eyes can be severely damaged by flying debris or simply by too much wind pressure. If you want your car windows open while you drive, open the driver's window wide, crack the others at the top, and be sure your dog's face is inside the car.

A final word about dogs and cars: Never leave a puppy or dog in a parked car for more than a few minutes. If your puppy is a valuable animal, you are inviting dognapping. Unfortunately, this is more common than you might think. More important, in all but the coldest weather (when your puppy could easily become chilled in an unheated car) your car will quickly turn into an oven if the sun hits it. The "greenhouse effect" of the sun on a metal car causes the temperature of the interior to go as high as 110 degrees in a very few minutes. A puppy's (or dog's) cooling system simply cannot handle that kind of heat, and the animal will soon suffer from heatstroke and dehydration, and undergo serious brain damage or die in a very short time. Don't take this chance. Even if you park in the shade, the sun will shift. If it is hot and you are going someplace where your puppy can't get out of the car with you, leave it at home and practice car manners in the evening.

During this entire month you have been continuing the early steps of Errorless Housebreaking. Somewhere around the ninth or tenth week of your puppy's life you may notice that it has more control over its sphincter muscles and that it almost always goes to one area to eliminate. As soon as it becomes obvious that your puppy knows when it needs

158

to eliminate and is able to wait until it reaches the desired area before it begins to urinate or defecate, you should begin to concentrate on showing it where you want it to go. All family members should be reminded to cooperate in this effort and learn to anticipate the puppy's needs.

9

Three to Four Months: Trying Things Out

At twelve weeks of age, your puppy has become firmly established in your household and has begun to understand what you want of it and to respond to you and your family. It is no longer confused and helpless, and has a lot more control over its own body than it did when you first adopted it.

Eager and Energetic

You will notice around this time that your puppy seems to have a lot more energy than it did before. It needs less sleep and is more alert and aware of everything going on around it.

Most puppies are very anxious to learn and to please their owners during this period of their lives, but they are often so restless and so easily diverted that it may be hard to make them settle down. You have to use a firm yet gentle hand. The section in Chapter 5, *Discipline: Reward and Punishment*, (page 93) will help you to understand

160

Table 17 HIGHLIGHTS CHART *Three to Four Months: Trying Things Out*

| | PUPPY DEVELOPMENT | | OWNER INVOLVEMENT | |
	Physical	Social/Behavioral	Puppy's Health/ Safety Needs	Working with Puppy Readiness
Three to Three and One-Half Months	Well-developed sensory/nervous systems	Testing/exploring Ready to learn more acceptable behaviors	Protect from harm, and exposure to disease† Space Management* Checkups, immunizations continued†	Discipline: Reward and Punishment* Needs new experiences to gain confidence and avoid future shyness—continue Socialization* Don't allow Jumping Up on People* Reinforce Car Manners*
	Attention span still short	Usually willing		
	More teething		Gradually go to 3 meals/day†	
Three and One-Half to Four Months	Usually has good control over elimination	Dominance/ submission with other dogs more pronounced	Regular grooming†	Continue Collar and Leash Wearing* Deal with Inter-dog Aggression* Reinforce Puppy Obedience* Begin teaching to Tolerate Human Absences* Reinforce Errorless Housebreaking*

* See *Detailed Discussion*.   † See Chapter 4.

how to do this. Remember that even though your three-month-old puppy understands more and is more capable than it was a month ago, its ability to concentrate is still limited to short periods of time, and training sessions must be paced according to your puppy's attention span.

A puppy this age needs to be protected against itself. Its very eagerness and energy can get it into serious trouble if you and your family don't anticipate its actions. More waking hours mean more time to get into things, and although a puppy this age has greater physical ability, it still has little if any judgment about physical danger. If you haven't done so yet, now is the time to double-check the safety and security of the puppy's space and of any other areas in the house or yard it may frequent.

It is important to continue to socialize your puppy to new experiences and people at this age. Your puppy will be very receptive to learning about new sights, sounds, aromas and sensations right now. Frequent car trips, introductions to new areas in the house, new sounds such as the vacuum cleaner, and so forth, are all valuable experiences for a three-month-old puppy. If you introduce it to as many new things as possible during this receptive age, it will offset the possibility of it becoming fearful of new things in the future when it is less able to handle them.

Your puppy's eagerness to get to know all about new people may get to be something of a trial if you allow it to greet every newcomer with its front paws firmly placed on the person's legs (or wherever your puppy's length permits it to reach). Now is the time to stop your puppy from jumping up on people.

Jumping Up on People

Freida was neatly dressed in her navy blue suit to go to her first job interview when she stepped outside into the backyard to say good-bye to her mother. Charlie, the family's Labrador, came galloping over to Freida and jumped up on her exuberantly before she could say "No!" Looking down at her now muddied skirt and torn hose, Freida burst into tears, while her mother fussed and wiped at her.

Jumping up on people in greeting is a happy, completely natural action of dogs that should be firmly stopped the minute it begins. Unfortunately, it is usually so flattering to owners—"He's so happy to see me"— that it is often hard for them to realize it can become a really annoying behavior, especially as a dog gets older and bigger.

Even if you don't mind your puppy jumping up on you, visitors to your house probably will not like having muddy footprints on their clothing or torn hose, and there may be times when, like Freida, you may not either. What is more, a fully grown large dog can knock a small child or a frail adult down if it catches them unaware or off balance.

HOW TO STOP A DOG FROM JUMPING UP ON PEOPLE

As with all behaviors you want to stop before they become habits, the time to stop a dog from jumping up on people is when it is a small puppy. This behavior usually begins when a puppy is around three months old, is full of pep and ginger, and is genuinely delighted to see you approach. But whenever it begins, take action to stop it right away.

The minute the puppy starts to put its front feet up on your legs, grap its front paws firmly but gently and hold on to them until the puppy becomes uncomfortable and wants to get down. Don't be rough but do hold the puppy's front paws tightly enough so that it can't squirm out of your grasp until it is ready to put all four feet on the floor. You may speak gently to the puppy while holding it. We say, "The puppy may get up on its terms, but it should get down on your terms."

Repeat this action every single time the puppy tries to jump up and ask other family members to cooperate. If children want to be greeted with a doggy kiss, tell them to get down to the puppy's level themselves but not to allow the puppy to jump up.

You may need to reinforce your "no jumping up" lessons when your puppy is around a year old and is approaching physical maturity. A dog this age has a great deal of energy, and it is also a stage in a puppy's life when it becomes stubborn and begins to challenge your authority. It can look upon jumping up as one way to establish dominance over you. Repeat the steps described above each time your puppy tries to jump up on you, and you will soon establish the fact that you will not tolerate this behavior.

When your puppy is thirteen to fifteen weeks old, it is time for another visit to the veterinarian for immunizations. The veterinarian can assess how well your puppy is growing and developing and, if you are feeding regular meals, may suggest that you gradually cut back on the number of feedings per day.

Regular grooming should continue throughout this month, and you may want to introduce more difficult grooming routines such as nail clipping. It is still too early for a puppy to be exposed to other dogs in a professional grooming establishment; however, if it is a breed that will require special grooming procedures, you may want to accustom it gradually to the tools or equipment that will be used.

Reinforcing Good Habits

All the good lessons you gave your puppy last month need to be continuously reinforced during this period of rapid learning. At this stage your puppy is even more ready and able to absorb verbal commands and understand physical restrictions. This is your opportunity to make those early lessons really gel.

As we said above, your puppy will benefit a great deal from frequent car trips at this age, which offers the opportunity to reinforce car manners. By the end of this month your puppy should be completely at home in the car and be able to behave, no matter what exciting event is occurring outside the car windows.

It should also be well into collar and leash walking at home. A good way to reinforce good leash manners is to have a family member try to distract the puppy with a noise while you are walking it in the house or yard. Do not try to distract the puppy by calling it or by using an obedience command (such as "sit"), however, or you will confuse it. If the puppy learns to behave well on a leash at home no matter what the distraction, it will stand both of you in good stead when it is ready to begin leash walking in public places.

All this time you are continuing with your daily puppy obedience sessions. Although, as we mentioned above, your puppy's attention span is still quite short, it is able to concentrate for longer periods of time as the month progresses.

By the end of this month most puppies are in complete control of their elimination. If you have followed the steps outlined in *Errorless Housebreaking*, your puppy is essentially housebroken. This does not mean it may not occasionally make mistakes, however, due to excitement or forgetfulness (its own or yours). After all, it is still very young. If this happens, do not overreact but check *Success?* on page 124.

Testing

Although your three-month-old puppy may be a delight most of the time, when it is about fourteen or fifteen weeks old its natural ebullience may lead it to test its powers over other household pets. It is feeling stronger and more in control of its own body, and it may decide to have it out with its canine housemate. This is when you need to understand the various kinds of inter-dog aggression so that you will know how to discourage it and can deal with it whenever it first occurs.

Inter-Dog Aggression

Other than aggression toward people, inter-dog aggressions is another major canine behavioral problem dealt with by professional animal behaviorists. It is a problem that has several facets: aggression between dogs (or sometimes a dog and cat) in a household; aggression on your puppy's part toward unfamiliar dogs outside the home; and aggression by another dog outside the home toward your puppy. In the first two instances, aggressive behavior on your puppy's part toward another dog may be fostered unwittingly by you, either by encouraging excess territoriality, by abetting overaggressive behavior through play (see *Nip Aggression in the Bud*, page 146), or as an outgrowth of your own or another family member's repressed aggression. It should also be emphasized here that castration of males may help a great deal to cut back on aggressive behavior toward other dogs, especially other males.

Inter-dog aggression can be very difficult to deal with, so let's take each type separately.

AGGRESSION TOWARD ANOTHER DOG
IN THE HOUSEHOLD

When Susie brought her Great Dane puppy, Samantha (Sam), home from college, her mother was upset and fearful that Sam would hurt her two-year-old Yorkie, Gladys. She was so fearful, in fact, that she took to closing Gladys up in her bedroom whenever Sam was in the house. Susie, on the other hand, insisted that Sam was as gentle as a lamb and that her mother was being much too fussy, was overreacting, and was being overprotective of Gladys, who she had always thought was a silly little dog. She went along with the separation even though it caused a tremendous strain on everyone in the household and entailed elaborate routines of closed doors and a great deal of shouting up and down stairs. Once, when Gladys had gotten loose and ran up to Sam, yipping and circling the big dog, Sam had growled and her hackles had stood up. This only served to make Susie's mother more determined to keep the dogs apart. One day, when Susie was at work and her mother had gone out in the yard with Gladys, a carpet cleaner inadvertently opened the door and let Sam out in the yard. As Gladys ran yipping up to Sam, the big dog let out a loud growl and attacked her, killing her instantly.

This is an extreme case that requires special handling because of the disparity in size of the two dogs. In this instance, all signs of aggression in either dog must be stopped. Inter-dog aggression within a household often occurs, and many times it is inadvertently intensified by an owner's repressed anger and actions.

Susie's mother had done exactly the wrong thing by constantly keeping the two dogs apart and not allowing them to get used to each other gradually, with supervision. At the same time, Susie's resentment and anger toward her mother (and her mother's pet, by

167

association) for being overly fussy and creating an impossible situation had been transmitted to her own dog, Sam. Each time she and Sam had had to go through the rigmarole of shouting and closing doors, Susie had seethed inside at her mother and her "stupid little dog." This repressed anger had been felt by Sam, who simply acted it out when given the opportunity.

Even though the repressed anger that Susie felt toward her mother and her dog was a contributing factor in this particular tragedy, there is little general advice we can give to avert such a situation except that you should do your best to recognize and deal with angry, aggressive feelings in yourself or in other family members and work hard so you will not transmit them to your pet. As to contributing actions: In the first place, Sam should have been immediately scolded and dominance-gentled (see *Nip Aggression in the Bud*, page 146) when she was still a puppy and first growled at the smaller dog. The two dogs should have been allowed to be together in the same room, with their owners, for part of every day, with neither one allowed to get away with an aggressive act. In this way they eventually would have become used to each other and have learned to tolerate each other's presence, even if they did not become friendly. By separating and isolating them, each time they met it was as two strange dogs.

In a case where two dogs, or a puppy and a grown dog, are about the same size and strength, it may be necessary to allow them to "rumble" a little, under supervision, in order for them to establish their roles as either dominant or submissive. It is best to allow them to get this out of their systems while someone is present, rather than when they are alone in the house. This can be a difficult task for an owner, but it is important not to separate the animals except in certain situations or they will never solve their differences. If the "rumbling" turns into a real battle, it may be necessary to intervene and help the younger, stronger dog win by reprimanding the older one. When there is a true age difference between two dogs, you may have to teach an old dog to stop fighting and help it to accept the submissive role. There must come a time when an old dog yields to a younger one in dominance-testing.

Some degree of inter-dog (or inter-pet) scrapping within a household is natural. Just as human siblings occasionally have spats, so will dog "siblings." This is all right and should not be cause for alarm unless blood is drawn and fur is flying. Although you must intervene immediately at any sign of real aggression, especially when a puppy is young, stop and look before you move to separate the dogs; often there is more noise than actual damage being done. If the scrapping becomes continuous, even after the dominant and submissive roles have been established, you may have to reprimand both dogs in order to get them to stop.

AGGRESSION TOWARD STRANGE DOGS

Eight-year-old Frank was peering out the front door of the lobby of his city apartment, holding his Boston terrier, Bimmie, on a leash. He was looking to see if the coast was clear of other dogs before they ventured out on the sidewalk. Twice before while he was walking Bimmie they had met another dog being walked on a leash, and Bimmie had lunged at the other animal, growling, dragging Frank behind. Once he had actually managed to grab a small cocker spaniel by the throat. The spaniel's owner had understandably been very angry, and Frank had been terrified. He had begged his father not to make him walk the dog anymore—at least until he became stronger and better able to control Bimmie—but his dad had laughed and said, "Good for Bimmie—he'll show them who's boss!" and had then reminded Frank of his promise to walk the dog before they had bought him two years ago. Even though Frank's mother is sympathetic toward the boy, she doesn't feel that it's right to contradict his father, especially when she's uncertain of just what to do. So, she stays out of the situation. Frank wishes now that they had never even gotten a dog.

Several factors are involved in this situation. In the first place, no one should walk a dog unless he has complete control over the animal. Second, if Bimmie had been properly trained to walk on a leash when he was a puppy, he would be less apt to try to break free, no matter what the provocation. And third and most important, Bimmie had been allowed to give his natural aggression toward other dogs free rein and apparently has even been abetted in this behavior by Frank's father.

Before a youngster is allowed, or asked, to walk a puppy alone, parents should be sure that both child and puppy have been properly schooled. This is not only in the interests of peace in the neighborhood but for the safety of both youngsters. A serious dogfight can be a dangerous thing for a child to get mixed up in; in addition, he might be badly hurt by being dragged by a large dog. Even if your own dog is small, its aggressive behavior may be directed at a much larger animal, and there is no telling if the other owner will be able to control his pet once it has been aroused to anger. It is up to the adults in the family to see to it that a puppy is taught proper leash walking (see *Leash Walking in Public Places*, page 190).

If a puppy learning to walk on a leash in public begins to act aggressively toward another dog, it should be corrected immediately by use of the dominance-gentling procedure (see *Nip Aggression in the Bud*, page 146). This may seem extreme, especially if you are on a public sidewalk, but it is the single most effective way to teach a puppy not to act aggressively. Even a capable youngster can perform this routine with a small puppy. If you are unwilling or unable to get down on the pavement when outdoors with your puppy, an alternative is to remove the puppy from the scene immediately while giving it a severe verbal scolding. Discontinue your walk, go home immediately, and confine the puppy for a while. Make it clear to your puppy that you do not approve of its actions. This must be repeated every time your puppy acts in an aggressive way toward another dog outside the home. Avoiding a confrontation with another dog by crossing the street or ducking into a doorway does not help. The tendency must be met head-on and the puppy shown, clearly and firmly, that you do not approve and that it will not be tolerated.

As we said before in *Nip Aggression in the Bud*, never hit or physically threaten a puppy that is acting aggressively and do not allow a child to do so. This will only lead the puppy to believe that aggression is all right and may very well incite it to increase its aggressiveness.

As to the attitude of Frank's father that Bimmie's aggressive behavior is not only all right but somehow commendable, someone in the family, probably Frank's mother, should have stepped in when the puppy was young, taken over his training, and also seen to it that Bimmie was castrated. Luckily, Bimmie is not a big dog, or a real tragedy might be even more predictable.

AGGRESSION TOWARD YOUR DOG BY ANOTHER OUTSIDE THE HOME

Pat was taking her poodle puppy, Missy, for a walk in the neighborhood when she noticed a large collie sitting on a front lawn. As she approached, the collie ran out and began to bark furiously. Nervous, Pat picked Missy up in her arms. The collie immediately redoubled its angry barking, ran up, and began to jump toward the puppy, snapping. Fortunately, the collie's owner ran out and grabbed it by the collar just in time, or both Pat and the puppy might have been badly bitten. Pat was very upset and decided that in the future she would carry a big stick with her, as a friend had advised.

Starting with the last sentence of this anecdote, the worst possible thing to do if you are out walking a puppy and are attacked by a larger dog is to threaten the attacker physically with a stick, club, your hand, or whatever. This will serve only to incite the aggressor and may result in serious physical damage to either yourself or your puppy.

For some reason that we do not fully understand, picking up a small dog also seems to trigger an aggressive response in a larger, potential canine attacker. Perhaps it is the sight of a helpless, dangling creature; whatever it is, it has an inciteful result.

If you are going to walk a puppy for the first time in a neighborhood where you do not know the dog population or if you are aware of the possibility of attack by other dogs, arm yourself with a water pistol filled with a vinegar and water solution. This is essentially harmless to other dogs but will cause them to retreat quickly. You can use it with impunity even if you are only vaguely suspicious of the advances of your next-door neighbor's German shepherd.

Even when walking your puppy in an area where there is a strict leash law you should be cognizant of the fact that many people let their dogs out—ostensibly only on their front lawns—and that some of these dogs may be potentially aggressive. It is always a good idea to be forearmed.

Dependence on People

Despite your three-month-old puppy's bluster and busyness, it is still very dependent on you for love, approval, and company. As it nears four months of age, it may become even more attached to you, seemingly aware of your every move and following you around the house at every opportunity. If you do not have another pet in the household, its dependence may become even more pronounced, and your puppy may have a difficult time letting you out of its sight. If you have not already begun to do so, now is the time to teach your puppy to tolerate human absence, or you will find yourself in a very difficult situation.

Helping a Puppy Learn to Tolerate Human Absence

When the Smiths moved to the country, Jane, the mother, did not know how to drive and stayed at home almost all the time with her youngest child and Phil, a small terrier that the family had adopted as a young puppy. When she went for walks, she took Phil with her. When the baby was old enough to go to nursery school, Jane learned to drive and went back to work. The minute that Phil, now three years old, sees Jane go to the hall closet he begins to whine and cry. When she starts down the stairs toward the garage, he sets up a high piercing whine. The next-door neighbors say the whine soon turns into constant hysterical barking that continues as long as Jane is away from home. It's obvious to Jane, too, that Phil has been vocal because when she returns he is very hoarse and can barely croak out a greeting. Closing Phil in the garage only seems to make him more anxious, and recently he has taken to scratching the doors so badly that they are beginning to splinter. The neighbors are becoming upset, and Jane and her family are considering finding a new home for Phil—one where someone will be at home with him most of the time.

Because a dog is a social animal, when it is adopted its human owner or owners quite quickly take the place of its mother and littermates. As we discussed in Chapter 5, dogs are very rarely alone in the world.

173

Even when they sleep by themselves, the rest of the pack is within calling distance, and a dog can usually smell and hear them. If a dog does find itself alone, it will usually whine, bark, or howl to reestablish contact with other pack members, and at the same time it often begins to run about looking for them.

This is the basis for what dog behaviorists call "separation anxiety" (a severe anxious reaction to being suddenly left alone, bereft of other members of the pack). Separation anxiety in dogs can lead to various types of "bad" behavior. When a dog becomes anxious because its owners are not at home, it usually tries to locate them by whining, barking, or howling. If this does not work, the dog begins to search for them, running from room to room. As it becomes more and more frantic and frustrated, the dog often chews on furniture and rugs, may knock things over, pulls its owner's clothing out of closets and drawers, and digs or burrows in the yard or the rug or sofa in an effort to get out and find its owners. Many dogs become so anxious that they also lose control and defecate or urinate in the house.

Although Phil has not exhibited all of these behavior problems, his continuous frantic barking and recent door scratching are symptoms of anxiety over separation from his human family or, in this case, from Jane in particular. He was apparently able to adjust easily to separation from other family members because they were not with him as constantly as Jane was. Jane was at home with him most of the time, and he was never conditioned to tolerate her absence.

Even though Phil even now can be successfully desensitized (become less sensitive to anxiety when deprived of human company) and can learn to accept Jane's daily absences, the process will take some time and effort, and will probably entail the help of an animal behaviorist. It would have been far better if he had been conditioned to the absence of human companionship early in his life as part of his socialization process.

Although those in a puppy's human family become surrogate pack members the moment it is taken away from its mother and littermates, a very young puppy sleeps a great deal and is usually confined in its "space" most of the time, so it is probably not acutely conscious of its owners' comings and goings. Somewhere around the age of three months, however, a puppy becomes increasingly aware of the people with whom it lives and of their presence or absence. It is probably allowed some freedom in the home because it is beginning to have bladder and bowel control, and it is apt to follow a favorite person around the house, to go to sleep at his or her feet, and seek out that person the moment it wakes. Simultaneously, a puppy's attention span is now usually rather well developed, and it may therefore be more aware of the passage of time. This is when you should consciously accustom a puppy to staying quietly in the house without you for longer and longer periods.

Some puppies seem to have little difficulty accepting owners' absences and appear to feel secure at home as long as there is a warm place to sleep and adequate food and water. Others become immediately anxious, whining and barking as soon as the owner is out of sight. Still others tolerate short absences and begin to be anxious only after an hour or two.

In many cases, severe separation anxiety does not surface until a puppy is grown or near-grown and is physically able to be left without feeding for eight hours or more. Boredom and loneliness can contribute to behavior problems when a dog is left alone for long periods of time (see *Boredom and Destructive Behavior* on page 226). Also, as we discuss in *Another Pet for Company?* (page 250), a companion pet can often help to offset a dog's loneliness and anxiety. But an owner can do a great deal to help a puppy grow up without

175

becoming anxious every time it is left at home without human company.

STEPS TO TEACH A PUPPY TO STAY QUIETLY AT HOME WITHOUT YOU

The trick is to let the puppy know that when you go out and leave it alone in the house, you will return, and that you expect everything will be in order when you do. We recommend several steps in order to achieve this. We call it conditioning the puppy; in other words, getting it used to remaining calm and quiet when separated from its human family or "pack."

To begin with, although we are in favor of taking a puppy out with you whenever possible in order to socialize it to all possible situations, you will have to begin to go out for brief periods of time and leave the puppy at home. You should do this even if you have nowhere to go; take a walk around the block or a ride to the post office or whatever, but do it on a regular basis. In a situation such as the one we described above, Jane should have left Phil home at least once a week when she went out for a walk.

We recommend that you go through the same routine each time you leave the house, even if it is only for ten minutes. Close the windows and lock the doors, turn on the lights, go to the closet and get a coat or sweater, pick up the car keys, and gather your bag or wallet or the baby—whatever you would normally take with you if you were going out for several hours. Your puppy will quickly learn to recognize the signs that you are about to leave, even when they vary with the season or time of day. So, think about what you normally would do if you were going out for the day and try to repeat those steps religiously, at least for a few weeks or until you're sure your puppy is on the right track to accepting your departure. If you have been regularly taking your puppy with you when you go out, it may become excited when you go through your departure routine. You may want to add some message to your routine, such as, "No, you're not coming with me" or just plain "No."

It's all right to say good-bye to the puppy if you are in the habit of talking to it, but don't make your good-bye too elaborate or you will succeed in making the animal think your departure is a big event. A simple "Be a good puppy," "Take care of the house," or "See you soon," will suffice.

It is important that you actually leave the premises. Don't think that your puppy won't know if you simply sit in the garage or the yard. The puppy will know you are nearby and may think that barking or whining will bring you back. The old theory of waiting outside the door to see what will happen and then bursting back in to punish a puppy if it barks is another example of what we call "negative reinforcement," which we discuss on page 238. All you accomplish with this ploy is to reward the puppy for barking by coming back. A puppy that is hungry for attention will not even mind the ensuing scolding that much!

When you return, even if only after ten or fifteen minutes, greet your puppy with a happy "hello," and immediately let it out in the yard or take it for a brief walk. Save your enthusiastic greetings until after the puppy has had a chance to relieve itself. Otherwise it may urinate from excitement. While it is out or when you return from the walk, look around to be sure that everything is all right in the house, and then make a big fuss over the puppy. Give it a lot of petting and possibly a food treat. If it was not good, take it to the point of infraction and immediately scold it (see *Discipline: Reward and Punishment*, page 93). Be sure to separate your coming home from any possible scolding or punishment, no matter how obvious the puppy's infraction may be, or your puppy will learn to be afraid of your homecoming and will hide from you every time you return. Always greet your puppy happily and let it out right away before you deal with any problems that may have occurred. Your homecoming should always be a cheerful occasion for your puppy.

Most puppies readily learn to accept owners' absences with equanimity, if not with pleasure, if they are conditioned at an early age. If a situation arises later on in a dog's life when an owner is home all the time due to illness or other change in circumstances, it may be necessary to desensitize or recondition the dog all over again, especially if either it (or the owner) has become overly dependent.

10

Four to Five Months: A Leveling Off

This month when your puppy is between sixteen and twenty weeks of age, seems to be something of a plateau for most puppies. Your puppy has undergone tremendous changes in the last three months, both physically and emotionally. Physically, from a vulnerable, helpless little wormlike being that could neither see nor hear nor walk nor eliminate without help and was completely dependent on its mother for warmth and sustenance, it has emerged into an active puppy that can walk and run, eat and drink, eliminate, chew, bark, and do all kinds of other things on its own. Emotionally and behaviorally, it has become an individual with its own personality, endearing qualities, and particular quirks. It has developed likes and dislikes, reacts to situations and people, and has formed strong attachments to its human family. It has learned a lot about what is expected of it as a pet. Most of the seeds of behavior that affect your puppy's personality as an adult dog have been planted by now.

This period in your puppy's life is a kind of leveling off, a time for the puppy to catch up with itself physically, and

Table 18 HIGHLIGHTS CHART
Four to Five Months: A Leveling Off

| | PUPPY DEVELOPMENT | | OWNER INVOLVEMENT | |
	Physical	Social/Behavioral	Puppy's Health/Safety Needs	Working with Puppy Readiness
Four Months to Four and One-Half Months	Continues teething and growing	Suspicious of new things/places; fearful Very curious	Three meals a day† Physical safety very important Checkups and immunizations continued† Continue to protect against exposure to disease†	Avoid sudden changes and harshness, be patient Continue to reinforce all previous lessons Continue to Teach to Tolerate Human Absence*
Four and One-Half Months to Five Months	Fully developed attention span in most dogs	Territorial awareness Beginning of overprotectiveness‡	Regular grooming† Play and exercise†	Control Excessive "Nuisance" Barking*

* See *Detailed Discussion*.   † See Chapter 4.   ‡ See Chapter 5.

digest what has gone before. Although a puppy does, of course, continue to grow and learn, everything seems to slow down a bit during this month—a marked difference from the rapid changes that preceded it and from the less rapid but important physical and behavioral changes that will follow.

Curious Yet Fearful

At about sixteen weeks of age or so you may notice a subtle change in your puppy. Although it is still very interested in everything and curious about new experiences, it may exhibit a slight hesitation in approaching unfamiliar objects and people. It may be less headlong in its exploration, a bit more cautious. Your puppy may not bounce back for more quite as quickly when reprimanded by you. It may seem to be going through a little more grown-up version of the fear period that it experienced when it was around eight or nine weeks old. This period usually lasts a very short time.

This is a very individual thing. If your puppy is at all reticent by nature, it may seem to almost step back and consider carefully before acting. On the other hand, if yours is a very outgoing puppy, it may continue to explore the world around it just as exuberantly as before.

Whichever type of puppy yours is, it is still very curious about the world around it and gains daily in its physical ability to explore further and further. Even a somewhat fearful puppy continuously amazes you by its seemingly endless activity, agility, and curiosity. Again, it is extremely important to rejudge and reassess the spaces in which your puppy is left alone, especially when you are not around, in order to prevent it from getting into trouble and hurting itself. Children should be reminded repeatedly to watch the puppy carefully, especially when it is allowed out of its room.

Keeping on an Even Keel

You have to gauge your interaction with your puppy carefully if it is at all fearful during this period. Hold off for a while on introducing brand-new experiences and wait a bit before starting a new training step or grooming experience, for example. Remind children that the puppy is still a baby and do not allow them to be overly rough or impatient.

Continue to reinforce all of the lessons you have already taught your puppy. At this stage especially, a puppy needs and craves the structure that familiar actions and reactions give it. It needs to know what to expect and what its limits are, and will only get this reassurance if you are consistent. Praise it lavishly when it is good (see *Positive Reinforcement*, page 213) and let it know that you love it even when it isn't.

Toward the end of this month you may notice that your puppy's attention span seems to have become longer. When you are interacting with it you may suddenly realize that it is less easily distracted and seems eager to continue with whatever you are doing. This is a good time to gradually increase the length of your obedience lessons.

This month of relative calm is a wonderful time to enjoy your puppy. It offers an excellent opportunity to solidify your relationship and give your puppy a lot of love and affection. Soon your puppy will be feeling more independent and adventurous again, so take advantage of this hiatus while you can.

Sometime during this month your puppy should visit the veterinarian for a continuation of its immunization series. Depending on how many immunizations your puppy has had so far, this may be the last in the series until it is grown. If so, your veterinarian may tell you that it is now safe for your puppy to go into public places. If this is the case, you can begin *Leash Walking in Public Places* (see page 190). If not, you will have to wait until next month when the series is completed.

Regular grooming should continue but, as we mentioned above, it is probably best to hold off for a while before introducing any new grooming procedures such as nail clipping if your puppy is at all fearful.

Play and Exercise

If yours is a small-breed or medium-breed puppy, it is more than half grown by now and no longer gets enough daily exercise by simply running around. It should begin to be exercised on a regular basis.

If its immunizations are complete, leash walking several times a day can form a major part of its daily exercise. If not, a regular play period is important. As we discuss in *Exercise and Play* (page 72) and throughout this book, daily play and exercise serve a much more important purpose than simply allowing a puppy to have fun. A healthy, active puppy needs the stimulation and refreshment of a daily workout in order to prevent boredom, restlessness, and subsequent "bad" behavior.

Most puppies are still too young to be pushed physically, however. While a puppy is growing its bones are soft and its muscles are not fully developed. Do not allow your puppy to become overtired, especially if yours is a very large or giant-breed puppy. Let your puppy set the pace and stop when it tires; and remind children to do the same. Remember: Never exercise a puppy or play with it vigorously for at least an hour after it has eaten.

Becoming Territorial

When your puppy is around eighteen to twenty weeks old it may suddenly have an increased sense of territory and begin to bark or growl when another animal or a person invades "its" yard or house. This will be especially evident if yours is an inherently territorial breed of puppy, such as a chow chow or corgi.

You must take special care to be sure your puppy's newfound awareness of territory and posessiveness does not develop into aggression at this point. If you have avoided fostering a sense of possession of objects or areas in your home in your pup (see *Nip Aggression in the Bud*, page 145), you may have to reinforce your lessons now. If your puppy becomes overly territorial with another pet in the household, continue to follow the steps outlined in *Inter-Dog Aggression*, page 166.

Even if your puppy does not become overly aggressive, it may begin to bark excessively whenever any creature (even a squirrel) approaches its property. While you would undoubtedly welcome a certain amount of warning barking from your dog, you most certainly want to immediately control excessive, "nuisance" barking.

Excessive "Nuisance" Barking

Mike was becoming more and more frustrated. He was trying to write a very technical report to take on a business trip the next day, and each time he got into it his miniature schnauzer, Pepper, began to bark continuously at someone walking by on the street. Sighing, he got up and opened the back door to the small enclosed yard. As soon as he sat back down, however, Pepper set up another round of continuous high-pitched barking that Mike could clearly hear even through the closed door. The neighbors would be understandably upset if this kept up, so Mike called Pepper back inside.

At this rate, he'd be up all night finishing the report and would be in no shape to make a good impression tomorrow.

It is natural for a dog to bark when someone or something encroaches on its property, and owners usually welcome this kind of warning barking. When a dog barks and barks continuously, however, it can be extremely annoying.

Continuous barking can be very difficult to control if you allow it to become a habit. It usually begins to be a problem when a puppy starts to be very aware of its territory—at around four and a half or five months of age. As with all other dog behaviors, it is far easier and more effective to teach your puppy at the onset that you will not tolerate this kind of excessive barking than wait until it becomes habitual.

HOW TO CONTROL NUISANCE BARKING

You can control excessive barking only when you are at home, but usually the dog that barks continuously when you are away from home has been allowed to form a barking habit over a period of time. If you teach your puppy not to bark excessively when you are at home, the lesson will carry over when you are not there.

The easiest and most direct way to stop a puppy that is barking too much is to distract it with a sudden loud noise. An empty coffee can can be made into a "rattle can" by filling it with stones and taping the plastic top back on. The minute your puppy begins to bark, shake the can loudly at the same time that you say, "No bark," firmly. The noise of the rattle can will momentarily distract the puppy from whatever is making it bark, and then your verbal message will be heard. If the puppy begins to bark again, repeat the action and the words. This method can be used both indoors and out. Repeat the action and words as a reminder each time your pet starts to bark too much. If this works well, it is all you need to do.

Many puppies, however, need more than this to stop them from barking too much. For these puppies, the best method is to show your displeasure by immediately removing them from the stimulus—whatever is causing them to bark—and isolating them from human interaction.

In order for this method to be successful you must follow a very specific routine. The minute your puppy begins to bark, say, "No bark," go and get it, and remove it from the stimulus. Carry or lead it to a small room such as a bathroom and confine it there. The area of confinement must be a neutral area; that is, it should not be the puppy's room or the room in which you feed the puppy or where it sleeps. It should never be a crate or cage.

The puppy may continue to bark as soon as you close the door. You should leave the puppy in the closed room for no less than three minutes and no more than fifteen. During this time the puppy will stop barking. When the puppy is *not* barking for about a minute, open the door and let it out. The timing may be a bit tricky because the puppy may stop for only a few seconds before it resumes barking, and the aim is to let it out only when it is not barking. Do not go into the room and get the puppy, but simply open the door and let it come out on its own. If your puppy has been very startled by this treatment, it may take a while for it to venture out.

When the puppy comes out, do not praise it. If it gets the idea that it will be praised simply for *not* barking, it may bark every time it wants attention just so it can then stop and be praised. Ignore the puppy for exactly fifteen minutes after you let it out, then interact with the puppy as usual, but still do not praise it. If someone comes into the house or room during this fifteen-minute waiting period, tell the person not to greet or talk to the puppy. For instance, you can tell children, "The puppy has been bad. Just ignore it until I say it's all right to pet it or speak to it." If the puppy begins to bark excessively again, repeat the entire confinement process.

One Month at a Time

This is a very effective method of stopping excessive barking for puppies that are social and outgoing, and like to be with people, It is neither effective nor desirable for a puppy that is timid or antisocial. If you have a timid puppy, you will need the help of a professional behaviorist to work out a method of dealing with excessive barking.

Confinement of this sort is not an effective tool for other kinds of behavior management and should not be used.

11

Five to Six Months: Beginning Independence

Up until now your puppy has probably followed you around the house, slept at your feet, and has been reluctant to let you out of its sight even when with you outdoors in the yard. When your puppy is somewhere between five and six months old, however, you may notice that it sticks to your side a bit less. It may wander off for short periods of time, into another room or part of the yard, only to return shortly. It is beginning to test out its independence.

Trying Things Out

Although your puppy is still not ready to go very far from the security of your presence, it is extremely active, energetic, and curious at this age. Its growth rate has slowed down a bit, and it has a lot of excess pep and vigor.

Left to its own devices, a puppy this age may get into difficulty, especially if it is strong-willed or stubborn. It may become even more territorial than before, and unless you have dealt firmly with aggression and nuisance bark-

Table 19 HIGHLIGHTS CHART

Five to Six Months: Beginning Independence

| | PUPPY DEVELOPMENT | | OWNER INVOLVEMENT | |
	Physical	Social/Behavioral	Puppy's Health/ Safety Needs	Working with Puppy Readiness
Five to Five and One-Half Months	Continues to grow and teethe	Very active, curious, and energetic Apt to be even more territorial‡	3 meals/day† Play and exercise increased† Checkups and immunizations continued if series not completed†	Begin Leash Walking in Public Places* Control Digging* Continue to reinforce all previous lessons
Five and One-Half to Six Months	Toys and small breeds almost full grown; large breeds more than half grown		Regular grooming†	Investigate Adult Obedience Classes*

* *See Detailed Discussion.*   † See Chapter 4.   ‡ See Chapter 5.

189

ing, which we discussed previously, you may begin to have a problem on your hands. It is important to be aware of any backsliding and immediately reinforce these lessons if your puppy shows any signs of testing you.

It is also important to continuously reinforce all the previous lessons in behavior and training you have given your puppy. Even though its attention span is now fully developed, a very energetic puppy is apt to completely forget its manners in the midst of headlong activity, and you may have to stop it and remind it regularly. Be sure to reinforce verbal commands on a daily basis.

Because it is so curious and active, a puppy this age benefits greatly from the new experiences it gains when it begins leash walking in public places. By the middle of this month its initial immunization series should be complete, and it is ready to venture out into the wide world.

Leash Walking In Public Places

Mary was dreading taking her three-year-old husky, Snowball, to the groomer to be bathed. She knew that after parking in the lot there were at least two blocks in a crowded downtown area to be negotiated. The first time she and Snowball had made the trip, she had had to apologize to at least six people for almost tripping them with the leash, and she had barely averted a potentially terrible scene with a large lady and her toy poodle. Snowball had decided that she wanted to see the poodle closeup and had dragged Mary across the sidewalk while the lady stood frozen, about to scream. Fortunately, a nice man had seen her plight and had grabbed Snowball's leash just in time. Mary had arrived at the groomer's trembling and exhausted and had persuaded the groomer on some pretext to stay late that afternoon so that she could pick Snowball up after the other shops had closed and most of the people had gone home. She had waited so long to make this appointment that poor Snowball looked like a mudball, but even now she wondered if she should have bothered at all. The whole thing was getting to be too much for her. She should never have gotten such a big, strong dog.

Mary's problem lies not in the kind of dog she has but in the lack of early practice she gave Snowball in walking on a leash in public places.

If a puppy becomes accustomed to wearing a collar and walking on a leash when it is very young (see *Accustom Your Puppy to Wearing a Collar and Leash*, page 151) and then becomes used to walking on a leash in public places as soon as it is ready to, it should be as easy to walk a Great Dane as a Chihuahua. Even if you live in the country or on a farm, you never know when the occasion to walk your dog on a leash may be a necessity, so do teach it leash manners or you will have the same terrible time that Mary did.

It is important for the puppy's sake as well as your own that it become a good leash walker. All puppies and dogs need the variety in their lives that going out for a walk on a leash provides, and they won't get it if they are difficult to walk. Even if you have an extra-large enclosed yard for your puppy, it eventually becomes bored and restless looking at the same scenery all day every day. It also becomes very wary, nervous, and overprotective of its property. No matter what the circumstances or the weather, all dogs should be taken outdoors for a walk every day of their lives and should be taken on longer expeditions to new places whenever possible.

TEACHING A PUPPY LEASH MANNERS

As soon as your veterinarian pronounces your puppy ready to venture out into the world, begin to take it out for walks. If you have practiced leash walking at home, the puppy will be perfectly comfortable wearing a collar and leash, and will know what is expected of it in the way of walking along with you.

The difference, of course, is in the distractions offered the puppy as soon as you leave home base. New sights, sounds, and smells, strange people, and other animals are intriguing, and your puppy is eager to investigate them all. To minimize these, begin your walks in your own neighborhood or block. It is a step in the right direction if your puppy has been socialized to a number of different people, has already learned how to act around strangers—not to jump up on them, nip them, and so forth—and has become accustomed to various sounds and sights by riding in a car. Nevertheless, all of the good lessons in leash walking that you have given your pet at home may appear forgotten the first time you and your puppy venture out.

There are two distinct kinds of leash walking that you will probably want to do with your puppy. The first is a casual stroll in your own neighborhood, nearby park, or playing field—the kind of walk you may take on a daily basis. In this type of walk you may want to allow your puppy to sniff and explore while you stand still holding the leash slackly. This is when a spring-retractable leash or an extra-long nylon lead comes in handy. It allows you to give your puppy some freedom without having to go into the bushes or tall grass yourself. As soon as you have had enough of this activity you can call your puppy back to you, shorten the leash, and resume your walk.

Your puppy must learn to respond immediately when called and to stay by your side without pulling when you have the leash shortened. This is the way it must remain when you are on a sidewalk with other people or animals, in a shopping mall or parking lot, a veterinarian's office or grooming establishment, or any other public place. It must also stay by your side if you are walking along briskly wherever you are; it must not suddenly lunge ahead or to the side no matter what the distraction.

The latter type of leash walking may be the most difficult to teach some dogs and can require a good deal of practice. An easily distracted, hyperactive puppy

192

does not automatically "get better" at leash walking as it gets older, however; it must be taught early and repeatedly.

When a puppy is young, it naturally wants to be with you and follow you. You can use this to your advantage when teaching your puppy to walk with you in public places. As you walk along, talk to your puppy continuously and remind it to stay with you. If a distraction such as another dog approaches, redouble your verbal encouragement. When your puppy begins to strain on the leash, snap your fingers or speak in a sharp tone to get its attention. If it tries to move off, stand still and let the pressure of the collar on the puppy's neck remind it that it has gone the limit. Then call it again, praise it for coming to you, and resume walking. Repeat these steps as often as needed until the puppy continues to walk with you and ignores the other dog (or whatever the distraction). Although most municipalities do not allow it, a dog that has been well trained to stay at its master's side ("heel") should be trusted to continue to do this without any leash at all.

Take your puppy to as many different places as possible as often as possible. Not only is this a valuable part of the puppy's socialization process, but it also enables it to learn how to behave in all situations—to stay by your side on a leash no matter what happens.

Play

While you are expanding your puppy's exercise program with regular leash walking, it is also important to give it an opportunity to play every day. If you haven't done so yet, this is an excellent time to teach it some games. The interaction with you is a welcome diversion for your puppy, and the added activity helps to tire it out and prevent boredom from setting in. Your puppy is ready for a great deal

193

more entertainment and diversion now that it is stronger and more energetic.

This is when troublesome behaviors such as digging may develop if a puppy is allowed to become bored and restless.

Digging

Digging is actually a symptom of boredom and destructive behavior, which is discussed in Chapter 14. It is not a common problem, but when it becomes a habit it can be extremely upsetting, especially if you value your plantings or the beauty of your grass.

Although some breeds of dog are known to be diggers by nature (dachshunds, for example), the cause of a digging problem is almost always boredom and lack of sufficient exercise. If an active puppy is closed in a yard in the morning and expected to stay quietly all day, it will become bored and restless. Something may trigger the idea to dig—an urge to get out underneath the fence, an enticing smell under the earth such as fertilizer, or a desire to uncover cool, moist soil to lie in if it is hot. Soon digging becomes a habit, and your yard begins to look like a mine field.

There are two things you must do to prevent digging from becoming habitual. First, recognize that the basic reason for destructive behavior is boredom and restlessness due to insufficient exercise. As a puppy grows and becomes more vigorous and physically strong, its need for daily exercise increases. This can happen so quickly that you may not realize you are not providing enough daily activity for your pet. Before you leave your puppy for the day, take it for a long run or walk, or play a vigorous game such as fetch for at least half an hour. Your puppy will then be relaxed, ready to sleep for a while, and less apt to become bored and restless during the course of the day.

Second, if you have allowed your puppy's digging to become something of a habit already, you have to show your pet that this is not acceptable behavior. The best method is to attach something unpleasant to the digging action. If you are at home and prepared to watch your puppy and catch its first sign of digging, you can then immediately rush outdoors while making a lot of very loud noise. Beat a metal pan with a spoon, shake a rattle can, shout, and yell. In other words, startle the puppy so that it stops in its tracks, then scold it firmly with a "No" or "No dig."

If you cannot stay at home and watch your puppy, you can prepare a "set-up" situation in which the puppy's own actions result in an unpleasant experience. As we discuss in *Inappropriate Chewing, Biting, Mouthing, and Pica* (page 140), this can be an excellent teaching tool. Bury something potentially noisy or startling, such as balloons that will pop, in the spots that your puppy likes to dig. Or put some red pepper or other unpleasant sharp-smelling and bad-tasting astringent-like substance just under the earth's surface. When the puppy begins to dig, the pop of the balloons or the bite of the pepper should prevent it from continuing. The only problem with this system is that if digging has already become a habit, you may have to booby-trap your entire yard or the puppy may simply find another spot to dig.

It is better to anticipate your puppy's needs before bad habits are allowed to develop and give it lots of exercise every day so that it does not become bored and destructive.

Ready for More Structure

If your puppy is a toy or a small breed, it is almost full grown at the end of this month. Large-breed puppies are more than half grown at six months.

Behavioral maturity still has a long way to go, however, no matter what the breed or size of your puppy. With advanced physical strength and stamina, a fully developed attention span, a lessening of its dependency on you, and a heightened sense of self, your puppy is ready for a bit more structure in its life. It is almost ready to learn how to behave as an adult dog should.

Now is the time for you to investigate adult obedience classes for your puppy. If you have attended puppy classes, you may have found that a class for older dogs is given by the same instructor. If not, find out where obedience classes are being held so that you can enroll your puppy. Ask your veterinarian, breeder, or local animal shelter, or look in the telephone book for an obedience school. Try to visit a class alone ahead of time so that you can be sure the instructor does not use harsh techniques.

Adult Obedience Classes

If you and your puppy have not been attending puppy obedience classes (see page 138), you should begin to investigate adult obedience classes when your puppy is about five months of age. Plan to start them when your puppy is about six months old; if you wait too long to start, your puppy will be much more difficult to teach.

Although some people do not agree with the importance of obedience school, we think it is a very necessary step in the puppy's upbringing. It helps your puppy learn how to be a well-mannered, responsive pet that knows what is expected of it. What is more, it teaches you how to teach your puppy what you want in the most effective way, without having to resort to harshness or anger. (It is important to stress again that you need to find an instructor who does not use harsh techniques.) This is especially important if your puppy's breed is at all aggressive or stubborn by nature or if your puppy will grow up to be a large dog. But even the tiniest toy will be a nicer, happier dog because of good early obedience training. Obedience classes bring structure to potentially unstructured situations, teach a puppy how

196

to react in the midst of other puppies that aren't trained, and help owners who know little about dog training.

Love alone is simply not enough. A puppy can love and be loved a great deal and still grow up to be an ill-mannered, unmanageable dog. A puppy whose owners rely simply on love and affection to teach it will be confused and probably unhappy as well. As we have said before, a puppy has no way of knowing what it is you want unless you are able to show it clearly. The best way you can demonstrate your love for your puppy is to provide a structure and easily understood limits for it. (Love = Limits and Structure.)

Your puppy will welcome the structure and order that going through obedience class gives its life. Just as a human child feels more confident when the adults around it are consistent and predictable, a puppy feels much more secure when limits are set. It is well worth the investment of time and money (neither of which is excessive).

12

Six to Seven Months: Adolescence

Your puppy's increasing sense of itself and awareness of the world around it becomes stronger this month. As it continues to mature physically, your puppy's personality becomes more pronounced, and you may be surprised to find that you are not always the center of its universe. Adolescence is beginning, and this may be the start of some upheaval in your puppy's relationship to you. The relative calm of the past few months is usually over sometime during your puppy's sixth month.

Preventing Problems

If you have located a satisfactory adult obedience class, begin classes now. Don't wait until your puppy is older to start; now is the time to teach your puppy proper behavior and to learn how to discipline it correctly without harshness or anger within the structure of a well run obedience class. Do this before next month when your puppy's new-found teenaged independence may lead it to believe it can

Table 20 HIGHLIGHTS CHART *Six to Seven Months: Adolescence*

PUPPY DEVELOPMENT		OWNER INVOLVEMENT	
Physical	**Social/Behavioral**	**Puppy's Health/ Safety Needs**	**Working with Puppy Readiness**
Six to Six and One-Half Months Possible first heat for toys and small females	More mature personality Asserts independence	Begin to feed 2 meals/ day—adult food† Discuss time for Spaying* with veterinarian Protect unspayed females against accidental mating Heartworm test/ medication, depending on season/ climate† Begin serious exercise routine† Regular grooming†	Begin Adult Obedience Classes* Continue to reinforce all previous lessons
Six and One-Half to Seven Months Baby teeth completely replaced by adult teeth (42)		Play† Deciduous tooth extraction if needed	Teach to Stay Away from Home* Begin professional grooming

* See *Detailed Discussion*.   † See Chapter 4.

get away with running you or can get a rise out of you by indulging in undisciplined behavior.

You can also help offset the development of many behavior problems that could begin during this unsettled period by providing your puppy with an even more rigorous daily exercise and play routine. Active breeds of dogs are now ready for serious exercise and need the diversion of new experiences. They should be taken on long walks or runs on a regular basis. As we point out throughout this book, not only does regular, vigorous exercise provide enjoyment and entertainment but it also tires out an active dog sufficiently so that little excess energy is left over for troublemaking.

Physical Changes/Health Care

A number of physical changes are evident in your puppy during this month, and you may want to discuss several aspects of its health care with your veterinarian.

TOOTH CARE

Sometime before seven months of age your puppy finally stops teething and its baby teeth should be completely replaced by adult teeth. An adult dog should have forty-two teeth, twenty-one on both the top and bottom of its mouth.

Occasionally this does not occur on time, and one or more baby (deciduous) teeth remain in a puppy's mouth, preventing the eruption of the adult teeth, or the adult teeth erupt adjacent to the remaining baby teeth. This happens most often with the large "canine" teeth (two large teeth on each side of both the top and bottom jaws). If this happens, the baby teeth should be removed because the condition can affect the puppy's bite and lead to future problems. Check your puppy's mouth from time to time, and if you notice that the adult teeth are not coming in properly, that there are two teeth in the same spot or there is redness or irritation in the gums, bring it to your veterinarian's attention.

Once your puppy's adult teeth are in place, discuss their cleaning with your veterinarian if you haven't done so before. Some dog breeds have a predisposition toward tooth and gum disease, and your doctor may want to schedule regular professional tooth cleaning for your puppy. Veterinarians are now actively encouraging dog owners to perform regular tooth cleaning at home as part of their grooming routine. Ask your veterinarian to show you how to do this. The sooner you get your puppy accustomed to this procedure, the easier it will be.

A CHANGE IN DIET

This is also the time to discuss with your veterinarian the switching from puppy food to adult dog food. Sometime around six months of age you may notice that your puppy leaves some food on its plate at each feeding. If it eats all of its meal, it may vomit shortly after eating or its stools may become very ample and loose.

Puppy food is extremely high in nutrients and is therefore very rich, and once a puppy's growth slows down a bit, it may not be able to digest it as well as it could before. When this happens it is time to switch to adult dog food. Even if your puppy is handling its food well, it should probably be changed over to adult dog food in the near future. Ask your veterinarian.

If you have been feeding your puppy on a self-serve, ad-lib basis, simply mix some adult food into its usual puppy meals, gradually adding more and more until the entire meal consists of adult dog food. If you have been feeding three meals a day, change over to two meals daily, gradually substituting adult dog food. You may find that your puppy wants a slightly larger quantity of food each mealtime to make up for the decreased nutritional density of the adult food. It is best to continue to feed the same form of food (that is, dry, canned, and so forth). Check with your veterinarian and use your own best judgment as to quantities to feed. See Chapter 4 for additional information.

HEARTWORM TEST/MEDICATION

A blood test for the presence of heartworms is usually given for the first time when a puppy is about six months of age or older. As we mentioned in Chapter 4, heartworms are transmitted from dog to dog via mosquitoes, so the exact time of the first test depends on the mosquito season where you live.

A blood test is always given before medication is prescribed because anti-heartworm medication can be harmful to a dog that is already harboring this parasite.

Even if you live in an area where mosquitoes are not in season, discuss the proper time for the test with your veterinarian when your puppy is around six months old. If you are going to be taking your puppy with you to a warmer climate, be sure to tell your veterinarian. Canine heartworm disease is extremely serious and often fatal, but it is easily prevented with a small expenditure of owner effort and money.

SEXUAL MATURITY IN FEMALE PUPPIES

Toys and small-breed female puppies may experience their first heat cycle any time from six months of age on. Especially with small-sized puppies, owners are often completely unaware of the onset of the first heat period. The flow is apt to be slight, and many puppies keep themselves so clean that there is little if any outward sign.

The first hint you may notice of this development is a sudden interest shown by neighborhood male dogs toward your puppy. If you have an uncastrated male dog in the household, he may suddenly begin to urine-mark and pester your female puppy, sniffing her and trying to mount her. It is imperative to protect your young female against accidental mating until you have her safely neutered. A six-month-old puppy is in no way suited for motherhood, either physically or emotionally.

No matter what breed or size female puppy you have, now is the time to discuss with your veterinarian the optimum age for a spaying operation.

Spaying (Neutering, Ovariohysterectomy, OHE)

When your female puppy is around six months of age you should talk to your veterinarian about when to have her spayed. The best time to perform the operation is anywhere from six to eight months of age, depending on the breed of puppy and her physical maturity.

For their own sakes, all female puppies should be spayed unless they are going to be bred. It does not matter how small a puppy will eventually be or whether it will ever be allowed outdoors unsupervised, the physical benefits of an early spaying operation are so great that there is no valid reason not to have it performed. In addition, you avoid several troublesome behavioral problems that are related to sexual drive in an unspayed female dog. As to the argument that spayed female dogs always get fat, this is simply not true. As a female puppy nears physical maturity she becomes somewhat less physically active and requires fewer calories for energy. This period of time usually coincides with a spaying operation, and therefore the spaying is often blamed if a puppy begins to put on weight. If you take care not to overfeed your pet and give her plenty of daily exercise, she will not gain too much weight. If you don't, she will get fat whether or not she is spayed.

PHYSICAL BENEFITS OF AN EARLY SPAY

It is simply not true that a female puppy should be allowed to have one heat or one litter before she is spayed. There are no benefits to be gained from waiting and many to be gained by an early spaying operation. A female dog that is spayed before her first (or second) heat has a greatly reduced risk of developing mammary gland cancer, the second most common malignancy in dogs. In addition, she will never develop an infection of the uterus. A uterine infection can become seriously life-threatening and require an emergency spaying operation. These infections very commonly occur in older, unspayed female dogs.

Of course, an early spay operation also prevents an unplanned, unwanted pregnancy. If your unspayed female puppy does become accidentally pregnant, you either have to have her spayed then, let her go through the pregnancy and have the puppies, or ask your veterinarian about the feasibility of giving her hormonal mismating shots, which can be risky. All of these options are potentially damaging to your pet's health, especially if she is very young. It is far better to have her spayed before being faced with these decisions.

BEHAVIOR BENEFITS OF AN EARLY SPAY

Although the behavioral benefits of spaying a female puppy are often less dramatic than those gained from castrating a male puppy, they are a definite positive factor.

Most unspayed female dogs have two heat cycles a year. During the first stage of the heat cycle there is a vaginal discharge. This may not be troublesome in some dogs, but it can pose a soiling problem for owners of those that bleed a great deal. Many female dogs become restless or irritable during this stage of the cycle or immediately after.

During the stage in the heat cycle when a female is receptive toward males, she may attempt to escape from the house. She may also indulge in territorial urine marking, especially if there are other dogs (male or female) in the household or immediate neighborhood.

An unspayed female may also suffer from a disorder known as "false pregnancy" which mimics all of the physical and behavioral stages of pregnancy even though there are no fertilized eggs. It is especially common in dogs that are very dependent on their owners, and can occur even when no mating has taken place. Some females go through a false pregnancy every time they come into heat and must then be spayed in order to prevent it from occurring again and again.

A very troublesome side effect of having an unspayed female dog is the necessity of keeping her away from male dogs and keeping them away from her. If you live in the country or suburbs, every time your female comes into heat, male dogs will appear on your doorstep, hang around your yard, try to get into the house, and fight with one another. To discourage this, you have to take your dog for walks far away from your house and even then remain constantly alert to protect her from roaming males. Many owners cannot deal with this and resort to boarding their pet in a kennel for the duration of each heat period—a troublesome and expensive procedure.

THE OPERATION

Although a spaying operation is quite routine, it is major surgery, which is another reason to have it performed when a puppy is young and heals faster.

After your puppy has been given a general anesthetic, a small incision (usually only one or two inches long) is made in her abdomen, and the uterus and ovaries are removed. The incision is then closed by stitches. Your puppy has to remain in the veterinary clinic or hospital for at least twenty-four hours after the surgery to be sure she has come out of the anesthetic and the incision is healing well.

When your puppy comes home she should be kept quiet for a day or two and allowed to resume activity at her own pace. She returns to the veterinarian's office in ten days or two weeks to have her stitches removed and the incision checked. After that she is completely recovered, and before long the incision becomes all but invisible.

Ready for New Adventures

In addition to being ready for adult obedience school plus longer and more exploratory walks and runs with you, your adolescent puppy is now physically and emotionally ready for some away-from-home experiences.

PROFESSIONAL GROOMING

If you are going to be taking your puppy to a professional groomer, now is the time if you haven't done so already. This is true regardless of whether your puppy is a breed that requires regular professional grooming throughout its life or if you have decided you simply want to take it to a groomer for a bath once in a while.

Even though your puppy's coat is probably not yet fully developed, the puppy should begin getting used to going to a grooming parlor and being left there for a while. It is important that your puppy's first grooming experience be as pleasant as possible, so visit several establishments alone before making an appointment. Explain to the owner or manager that you are going to bring your puppy in for a visit, to be bathed or simply brushed and combed, and you plan to leave it for only a short time. Most proprietors are happy to participate in this initial introduction.

Ask to be allowed to see the groomer at work. You can tell a great deal by the way the dogs react to the groomer and the way the groomer reacts to them. While many dogs do not actively enjoy a grooming session, if they trust the groomer most will stand quietly with no cringing or growling. Do not leave your puppy with any groomer who appears impatient or harsh.

When you return to pick up your puppy, it should be lively, normal-acting and happy to see you. If it is very quiet, glazed-looking, or seems dopey, suspect that it may have been given some kind of medication to keep it quiet. This should not be necessary for any puppy, and you should find another grooming establishment.

BOARDING YOUR PUPPY

This is also the right time to begin accustoming your puppy to boarding, whether or not you expect to kennel it on a regular basis. Again, the earlier your puppy becomes used to a variety of experiences, the easier it will be for both of you.

Learning to Stay Away from Home

Marie is single and has seldom gone away except for occasional weekend trips. In the past when she visited her sister and husband in the country, she always took her cocker spaniel, Susie, with her. Now, Marie's sister and husband have just invited her to go to Europe with them for three weeks. She really wants to go but is afraid she will have to say no because she has no one to look after Susie and knows the dog, now eight years old, would be traumatized if put in a kennel for the first time. Her sister is understandably annoyed, and despite herself, Marie is beginning to feel quite resentful toward Susie.

It is an important step in a puppy's socialization process to learn to stay in a boarding kennel without undue stress. No matter how unlikely you now think it is that you will ever board your pet, you never know when an opportunity to go away may come up or an emergency may arise that would entail leaving it. There is bound to come a time when your dog has to be separated from you, away from home. It is far better for it to learn to accept this without trauma as a puppy than be faced with Marie and Susie's problem later on.

As soon as your puppy has had all of its immunizations and your veterinarian says it is all right for it to be exposed to other dogs, it's time to introduce it to boarding away from home. Ask your veterinarian, the breeder from whom you got your puppy, or a responsible dog owner for a kennel recommendation. The American Boarding Kennel Association (ABKA), an organization devoted to providing good boarding care for pets, provides accreditation to boarding kennels that meet a high set of standards. Membership and accreditation in the ABKA mean that a kennel operator is serious about his or her responsibility toward pets and pet owners. For a list of member kennels you can write to the American Boarding Kennels Association, 4575 Galley Road, Suite 400-A, Colorado Springs, CO 80915.

Before boarding your puppy for the first time, visit one or more boarding facilities. Talk to the owners or managers and ask to be allowed to look around. Obviously, you want to choose a clean, well run facility for your puppy. Kennels vary widely in their accommodations, from those that are extremely stark and functional to some that provide a living-room-like atmosphere for their charges. More important than fancy trappings is the attitude of the caretakers toward their charges. You can tell a great deal by observing the dogs' reactions to the kennel workers as they go about their business. Ask about special care and/or feeding in case it is ever necessary, and ascertain what arrangements have been made for emergency veterinary care should it be needed.

A responsible boarding kennel does not accept any animals that do not have up-to-date immunizations, and many also require a veterinarian's certificate stating that a dog is in good physical health.

Once you have decided on a boarding kennel, tell the

owner or manager what you have in mind. Explain that you want to accustom your puppy to boarding and that initially you will be leaving your pet for only one day.

A responsible kennel proprietor should be only too happy to help you accustom your puppy to staying in his facility. If all goes well and your puppy rejoins you in a happy, healthy condition, repeat the one-day stay in a few months. If not, try another kennel. After a few daytime "dry runs," try an overnight stay.

If an occasion to board your puppy does not come up in the next six months or so, it is a good idea to repeat a one-day or overnight stay anyway from time to time—once a year is probably enough when the dog is an adult—so that your pet never forgets that everything will be all right and that you will return for it when you leave it in a boarding kennel.

Some very sociable dogs seem to enjoy boarding away from home from time to time while other dogs learn only to tolerate it, but a dog that has been conditioned to it will not be unduly traumatized by staying in a kennel if it becomes necessary.

13

Seven to Eight Months: Becoming a Teenager

As your puppy matures both physically and behaviorally during this month, it often seems to be on the brink of adulthood. But, like a human teenager, it can change almost hourly from calm, well-mannered, predictable behavior to babyish ways. It may seem to forget everything it has learned in previous months and can appear to be deaf or dumb when called or given a familiar command.

Testing

Just as some human children go through the teen years with their parents in relative harmony and calm while others seem to be in a constant state of upheaval, the degree of testing and rebellion that your puppy goes through at this stage of its life is highly individual. A lot depends on your puppy's basic temperament and personality. It also depends in a large part on how well you have laid the groundwork for a good relationship and have

210

Table 21 HIGHLIGHTS CHART

Seven to Eight Months: Becoming a Teenager

| | PUPPY DEVELOPMENT | | OWNER INVOLVEMENT | |
	Physical	Social/Behavioral	Puppy's Health/ Safety Needs	Working with Puppy Readiness
Seven to Seven and One-Half Months		Seems to forget everything previously learned; reverts to "babyish" ways	Feed two meals/day† Increase play, exercise† Regular grooming† Protect unspayed females against accidental mating	Firm hand needed Positive Reinforcement*
		May challenge your authority—testing‡ Lack of attention		
Seven and One-Half to Eight Months			Discuss time for Castration* with veterinarian	

* *See Detailed Discussion.*   † See Chapter 4.   ‡ See Chapter 5.

211

given the puppy the structure it needs at this time in order to know what is expected of it.

But no matter how well you have taught your dog and how well it has responded to you, you may be in for some surprises. Depending on its particular personality and size, your puppy may indulge in several different types of nonresponse. When you call it to come for a grooming or training session, for instance, it may pay no attention or pretend that it doesn't hear you at all and go right on doing whatever it has been; it may get up and walk or run in the opposite direction; it may decide that now is the time for a game and run around barking frantically; or it may simply stare at you defiantly.

The variations are numerous, but whatever your puppy does or does not do, it should be obvious to you that it is challenging your authority. If it could talk, it might say something fresh, such as "You can't make me do what you want. I'm busy now."

The Velvet Glove

You must not let your puppy get away with ignoring or defying you for one minute, or you will be setting a dangerous precedent that will be very difficult to break. Don't let it feel it can respond to your wishes when it gets around to it, but make it very clear that you mean business. Stay calm, but be very firm.

This is an extremely important time to remind your puppy that you are still its pack leader and will continue to be. You must immediately act and reinforce or even reteach all of the previous lessons that you have given your puppy. At the same time, remind it continuously that you love it and that you expect it to behave within the framework previously laid down.

Don't let your annoyance and frustration at your pup-

212

py's sudden defiance allow you to forget, however, that praise is a powerful training tool. Always act quickly to correct your puppy when it misbehaves or defies you, especially during this often rebellious stage, but don't forget to let it know how pleased you are when it does well.

Positive Reinforcement

It is axiomatic that people usually don't trouble to communicate when everything is going well but reserve their comments for complaint or criticism. Your puppy has no way of knowing when it is doing well or when you are pleased with it unless you tell it so repeatedly; it cannot match a "no comment" with approval.

Positive reinforcement is no more or less than reinforcement for good behavior that you give your puppy. It may seem simple and obvious to reward a puppy with a pat, hug, or "good dog" when it behaves, but this valuable teaching tool is often overlooked by owners. This is especially true as a puppy matures and has learned the basics of good behavior; at this time it is easy to take your pet's proper actions for granted and to assume that nothing more is needed.

Many behavior and training problems arise just because an owner fails to understand this. For example, you may not praise a puppy when it has behaved well in your absence (has not chewed anything or soiled the house, for instance), but you scold it when it has misbehaved. Your puppy may well become confused and get the mistaken idea that the only way to capture your attention is to misbehave.

That is why we continuously repeat phrases such as "tell your puppy that it is good" and "praise your puppy when you come home and find that all is well." We are not simply suggesting that you be nice to your puppy. Praise and reward (reinforcement of good behavior) are necessary to teach a puppy how to behave

213

and to remind it that it is doing well and pleasing you—no matter how old it is. In addition, your puppy needs constant praise when it is doing the right thing so it can deal with new circumstances and situations that might otherwise confuse it or tempt it to lapse into unacceptable behavior.

Continue to increase your puppy's daily exercise and play times, or perhaps begin to have more than one exercise and play session each day. You should gauge your puppy's exercise needs by its stamina and activity level and the amount of "ginger" it still has at the end of a session. Although you should stop when your puppy is obviously tired, remember that a well-exercised puppy has little energy left over for mischief. More about this in the next chapter.

More Health Concerns

As your puppy continues to develop sexually, you must remember to protect your unspayed female from accidental mating.

Your male puppy will soon become sexually mature, and now is the time to think seriously about castration and to discuss with your veterinarian the appropriate age for the operation. If you are in any doubt about the advantages of castration for male dogs, read the following section carefully.

Castration, (Neutering, Altering)

Not too long ago castration was usually performed on male dogs only for remedial reasons, but more and more it is becoming routine as preventive surgery. Early castration for male dogs that are not going to be

214

bred helps to avoid many future physical and behavioral problems.

You may very well hear a number of arguments, sometimes passionate, against having your male puppy castrated; these people think it is "cruel," will make the dog a less able watchdog, and (the old bugaboo) will make him get fat. Many people who have no qualms about spaying a female dog feel that castrating a male is, somehow, a bad thing to do and is certainly unnecessary.

To answer these arguments briefly: The operation itself is certainly not "cruel" but is fairly simply and routine. When done on a young dog, it entails at worst one or two days of discomfort. As to cruelty of a different sort—mental or psychological anguish—dogs simply do not know the difference since they have no awareness of their sexuality, per se. A castrated dog will be the same caliber of watchdog as he was before the operation. He may simply be less aggressive in some areas, especially toward other male dogs; after all, females make good watchdogs too. He will not get fat if he is given a good, balanced diet and enough exercise. As to the operation being unnecessary, your own informed judgment, based on the benefits we outline below, should decide that. Don't let well-intentioned friends talk you out of it.

You should discuss castration with your veterinarian by the time your male puppy is seven months of age. Depending on the size and breed of a dog and its stage of maturation, the operation is best performed when the animal is young—somewhere between six months and a year and a half—although it can be done at any age in a dog's life.

PHYSICAL BENEFITS

Intact (uncastrated) male dogs are subject to a number of hormone-related medical problems as they age. They may develop prostate, perianal, and testicular infections and tumors. All of these disorders are dependent on testosterone, the male testicular hormone, and castration is routinely performed in the course of treating them.

In addition, unaltered male dogs are much more prone to roaming and fighting than castrated ones. These behaviors are potentially more physically dangerous than hormone-related disease. Thus, you will be protecting your male puppy against physical disease and danger by having him castrated when he is young.

BEHAVIORAL BENEFITS

Castration is also particularly effective as a preventive measure against a number of common behavioral problems.

One of the most troublesome aspects of male canine behavior is aggression against other dogs. As a male dog reaches full physical and sexual maturity, he becomes more and more protective of what he considers "his" territory. His definition of "his" area tends to change, and the boundaries enlarge, until sometimes an entire square block or country mile falls within his radius. Often, owners are not aware of the degree of territoriality that has developed in a pet until a tragedy occurs and another dog is severely hurt or even killed. "But he's always so gentle" is a common cry of an upset owner in these circumstances. And he is—until another male dog invades property that he considers his own. Then his male territorial instincts override any "social" behavior he may have learned, and he defends his turf to the death.

Along with this territorial instinct comes, of course, roaming behavior. A sexually active male dog must patrol the boundaries of his property and constantly widen them. In addition, he is always on the lookout for receptive females and, if there is a bitch in heat within many miles, he will find her. Often, a male dog hangs around the area for days on end, apparently forgetting that he even has a home. Terrible dogfights can occur when several males converge on a bitch in heat, even if she is confined indoors, and the resulting veterinary bills may be staggering.

Even if you have an uncastrated male dog that is never allowed outdoors alone and is, therefore, probably not going to get into fighting or roaming difficulty, he still may indulge in territorial urine marking—raising his leg on every upright surface he can find. This can occur seemingly out of the blue but is usually related either to a female coming into heat somewhere within his range or another male dog moving into the neighborhood. You may not be aware of either occurrence, but you will soon know it by the fact that your well-housebroken pet has suddenly "broken training" and is marking up your house. In the absence of other male dogs, housebound males may also take out their aggressive territorial protection on humans. Overprotectiveness of family members may manifest itself in growling at, and even nipping, visitors to your home. (See also what we are calling *"Negative Reinforcement,"* page 238.)

Other sexually related behaviors of male dogs can include mounting human legs, climbing up on people, especially children and girls, and even knocking children down and climbing on top of them. This is especially frightening and dangerous if a dog is large.

All of these behaviors can usually be corrected by a combination of castration and training, but it is difficult to break a habit that has become ingrained. That is why we strongly suggest early castration for all pet male dogs.

THE OPERATION

The operation itself is relatively simple, especially if it is performed when a dog is young. It does require general anesthesia, and a dog is often kept in the hospital overnight until he is fully recovered from its effects, although sometimes a dog is discharged the same day as the operation.

217

One Month at a Time

The scrotum is usually left intact and the testicles removed through a small incision. There are generally no complications, and the incision heals within a week. After a month or two the scrotum usually shrinks and is covered with hair.

14

Eight to Nine Months: Gaining Independence

Now that your puppy has begun to learn that it can not only survive without you but can also function quite well on its own away from home, it begins to feel more and more independent. Your puppy has probably outgrown its brief teenaged rebellious period with the help of your firm hand, but even if it is more willing to pay attention to you and more compliant with your wishes, you may notice that it is becoming increasingly ''antsy,'' restless, and territorial.

Increased Sexuality/Restlessness

Your middle- to large-size female puppy may experience her first heat cycle sometime during this month. Again, we must stress the importance of keeping her isolated from all male dogs, even if you only suspect that she may be receptive, in order to prevent accidental mating.

Your male puppy soon starts to lift his leg to urinate instead of squatting. This is a sign that he is becoming

219

Table 22 HIGHLIGHTS CHART
Eight to Nine Months: Gaining Independence

	PUPPY DEVELOPMENT		OWNER INVOLVEMENT	
	Physical	**Social/Behavioral**	**Puppy's Health/ Safety Needs**	**Working with Puppy Readiness**
Eight to Eight and One-Half Months	Possible first heat for medium to large females		Feed two meals/day† Protect unspayed females against accidental mating	Continue Positive Reinforcement*
	Leg lifting can begin with males	Territorial "marking" may occur—males		Deal with inappropriate elimination (*see* Errorless Housebreaking*)
Eight and One-Half to Nine Months		May begin to escape and roam	Increase exercise and play† Protect from harm Regular grooming†	Avoid Escaping/ Roaming*
		May exhibit destructive behavior		Prevent Boredom and Destructive Behavior*

* See *Detailed Discussion.*   † See Chapter 4.

sexually mature. At first you may find it amusing when he wants to lift his leg on every blade of grass in your yard or on every upright surface he comes across when you are walking him, but your amusement may soon turn to annoyance, especially if he decides to "mark" everything inside the house as well as out. Keep a sharp eye out for this. Sometimes it is not very noticeable because your puppy is able to squeeze out only a few drops of urine on each object, and it is easy to overlook until either the odor or the resulting stains become evident. You must not assume because your puppy has been well trained until now that he won't indulge in marking, especially if there are other dogs (or even cats) in the household or in the immediate neighborhood.

This behavior is less common in females than in males, but your unspayed female puppy may suddenly engage in urine marking when she comes into heat. The ensuing puddles are usually more obvious than the drops left by a leg-lifting male puppy, but some females also go from place to place leaving small amounts of urine in each, so you should be alert to this possibility. Again, this happens most often when there are other dogs living in the household or on neighborhing property.

This type of urine marking in both males and females is directly connected to the increased territorial feelings that go along with sexual maturity. As we discuss in *Errorless Housebreaking* (page 119), neutering usually puts a stop to excessive urine marking in both males and females. Until that can be done, however, you have to firmly reinforce your original housebreaking. Don't fall victim to the notion that your puppy's sudden inappropriate urine marking (or any other type of inappropriate elimination) is just a "stage" and will go away by itself. No matter how well housebroken your puppy has been in the past, any sign of slipping should be corrected immediately or it will become a habit that is much more difficult to break.

221

Other manifestations of an increased sexual drive and its accompanying territoriality may be a recurrence of excessive "nuisance" barking, and some males may again exhibit aggressive behavior, especially toward other dogs. Any signs of these or any other overtly territorial behavior need to be dealt with right away.

Severe restlessness can also develop along with these problems. This is especially true if yours is a strong, very active breed of puppy. Your puppy may begin to indulge in escaping/roaming behavior.

Escaping/Roaming

Josie had a plane to catch. While she was packing, she put her two-year-old Labrador retriever, Bill, out in the fenced yard for a run before she took him to the kennel. With an hour to spare before she had to leave for the airport, she went to get Bill to take him for the short trip to be boarded. Looking out, she was horrified to see that he wasn't in his yard and wasn't in sight anywhere. He had again jumped the fence of his yard and taken off. She backed the car out and began the now familiar, slow drive around the neighborhood, stopping to call every half block. If she didn't find Bill soon, she'd miss her plane. Near tears, she had just vowed that she would leave him wandering around—it would serve him right if he was picked up and put in the pound—when she saw a familiar black shape trotting happily along the side of the road, tail waving in the air.

Escaping and roaming are very common problems, especially for country and suburban dogs that are regularly confined to runs and yards. Large dogs, uncastrated males, and breeds that require a great deal of exercise are particularly apt to become escape artists. Very strong dogs often wander many miles before they are found or are picked up by someone. Escapers and roamers not only become neighborhood nuisances, dumping over garbage and getting into other mischief, but also often fall victim to accidents and poisonings. In municipalities where there is an active dog-control program, roamers are often picked up and impounded and their owners assessed with stiff fines if they are lucky enough to be located. It is not uncommon for a "lost" dog to be impounded and put up for adoption because it has no identification and its owners cannot be reached.

Although owners build stronger and stronger and higher and higher fences, they are often completely defeated by a determined dog. The more often the dog manages to escape, the harder it tries the next time. Left unchecked, escaping and roaming behavior soon becomes a deeply ingrained habit that is extremely difficult to break.

AVOIDING ESCAPING/ROAMING

Dogs usually escape from their yards and roam for one or more reasons. They are bored and lonely and looking for a little excitement. They are not getting enough vigorous physical exercise. Or, if they are males, they are indulging in territorial sexual behavior or looking for a receptive female.

Rather than try to beat a determined adult dog at the escaping game, think about its ends while it is still young, before escaping and roaming become habitual.

As we discussed in the previous chapter, castration removes one of the most compelling reasons for escape and roaming in male dogs. It can even be somewhat effective when performed on an adult dog that already is a roamer, but as we said, roaming behavior can quickly become a hard-to-break habit. It is far easier to prevent it from occurring in the first place, when a dog is young.

That is step one. Even a castrated dog may take to escaping and roaming, however, if it becomes bored enough, especially if it sees something interesting outside the fence. You should realize that it is not enough

223

to provide a dog with a fenced yard and shelter and nothing to do all day. In *Boredom and Destructive Behavior*, page 226, we talk about some of the things you can do to keep a dog from becoming so bored that it feels it has to escape and run around to find something to do. Another dog for company may also help (see *Another Pet for Company?* on page 250.)

There are some breeds of dogs, especially the hounds, working, and sporting breeds, that require above-average amounts of daily exercise in order to stay calm and quiet for the rest of the day. You must recognize this if you own one of these breeds and provide it with a lot of daily, vigorous exercise before you confine it, or it will soon develop a roaming habit out of physical need.

If you begin early enough to provide a puppy with enough stimulation so that it doesn't have any desire to escape from its yard and roam, you are many steps ahead of the game. But no matter what you do, some puppies are simply never happy until they see what is on the other side of the fence. If you notice that your puppy is beginning to show an interest in getting out of its yard, either by trying to go over or under the fence, try to nip the tendency in the bud right away. Paving stones or other large stones placed along the inside bottom edge of a fence usually prevent a puppy from being able to dig underneath. Of course, a very high fence can prevent a puppy from jumping out, but this may not be practical or permissible in your area. If a puppy has already proudly demonstrated to you that it can get over the fence, act right away to stop this from becoming a habit. Take a piece of heavy cardboard (the side of a carton, for example) and tie it across your puppy's shoulders, bringing the string underneath the dog's body, behind the front legs or secure it in place with a harness. This is another example of effective punishment that a dog brings on itself: When it tries to get into position and crouch to jump, the cardboard will poke it and hurt. Be sure to try this only when you are at home and checking the puppy regularly, however, because it could easily become tangled in the string or harness.

More Activity

There are a number of different kinds of activity that you can engage in with your puppy in order to prevent it from roaming the countryside for excitement.

In addition to walks in the neighborhood, your puppy will enjoy car trips to other locations for a change of scenery once in a while.

Some puppies really enjoy running. Even tiny toys have a lot of energy and often find running with a human great fun. If you or another family member jogs or runs regularly, think about the benefits of taking your puppy along with you once or twice a week. If you follow safety rules and always keep your puppy on a leash, running can be an excellent source of enjoyment and enhanced good health for both of you. If your puppy is a small or medium breed, its skeletal structure is probably able to withstand the stress of steady running at around eight months of age; larger dogs should not begin regular running, especially on pavement, until they are about a year old, and giant breeds even older. Always have your puppy checked over thoroughly by your veterinarian before you embark on any serious exercise or training program with it. Tell your veterinarian what you have in mind, and be sure that your puppy's cardiovascular system, skeletal system, feet and pads are in tip-top shape before you begin.

In addition to preventing your puppy from wanting to escape and roam, plenty of exercise and activity keep your puppy from becoming destructive.

Boredom and Destructive Behavior

The Petersons are at their wits' end. Their fifteen-month old Irish setters, Mac and Mabel, have become so destructive that first their house and now their yard look like disaster areas. When the dogs first began to chew and scratch, they closed them in the basement. Soon the animals had demolished all of the furniture, rugs, and even the floors and walls in the basement. The Petersons decided to enclose a run in their yard so that Mac and Mabel could stay outside during the day. Now the run is pitted with holes, and there isn't a green thing in sight. Having been told by the breeder that two dogs would entertain each other, they feel that they were duped, that two dogs simply make more of a mess than one! No matter how much they scold them and discipline them by keeping them confined even when they are home, the dogs continue to destroy house and yard. They always take the dogs for a long walk when they get home from work and leave them some toys to play with. They are completely bewildered as to what to do next, short of giving the dogs away.

Tanya, a year-old Lhasa apso, is hardly ever left alone except when her family goes out for dinner, which they like to do three or four times a week. Then she chews on the carpet. Recently it has gotten so bad that she has actually chewed holes in some spots, and the Martins have had to move the living room furniture to cover them. They have tried scolding her and have recently begun to close her in the bedroom, but now she's starting to chew the bedspread and chair slipcovers.

What many owners do not seem to realize is that destructiveness in dogs is almost always directly related to boredom, which is exacerbated by confinement and lack of exercise. Destructive behavior can surface when a dog approaches full growth and its attendant vigorous energy level. When an active "teenaged" dog first be-

226

gins to equate its owners' absence with long, boring hours of nothing to do, trouble can begin. Owners often wait until the problem becomes really severe, however, before they recognize it and seek help.

Because Mac and Mabel are sporting dogs, they require a great deal of exercise and are especially sensitive to being closed in small spaces. Even each other's company palls after a while, especially in a confined area, and they soon run out of acceptable things to do. Small dogs such as Tanya require less exercise, but if they have become used to having people around all the time, they may become bored very quickly when left on their own with nothing to do. Neither Mac and Mabel nor Tanya can be broken of their destructive habits by scolding because they are not really being "bad" but literally cannot stop themselves from doing something to relieve their intense boredom and the tension that results from lack of sufficient exercise.

What can their owners do, then, short of allowing them to destroy the entire house and yard? The best solution for all dogs, but especially for those that require a lot of daily exercise, is to wear out the dog (or dogs) *before* you go out. We like to say, "Break the dog before you leave." If Mac and Mabel are worn out with a vigorous play and exercise routine before the Petersons go to work, they will sleep more and be much less apt to become destructive. This may require some change in the Petersons' morning routine, but it is worth it if they want to keep their dogs. Tanya should also be given a good long walk or vigorous play session just before the Martins go out to dinner. Because she is small she will then probably sleep almost the entire time her family is out.

Another trick to help offset boredom is to have a special toy that you give to the dog only when you are going out. It should be something that the dog has already shown an interest in and liking for—a particular kind of non-harmful chew toy, for instance—but it should be a new and especially desirable example of its type. Give it to the dog *only* when you are going to be out, and take it away as soon as you return. A caution here: As we mention in *Inappropriate Chewing, Biting, Mouthing, and Pica* (page 140), if you give your puppy a rawhide chew toy in your absence, make a point to check that the puppy is not biting off and swallowing too many pieces of rawhide. If it is, you have to substitute another kind of toy or a larger rawhide chew that is harder to break pieces from. If the object wears out or seems to lose its charm from time to time, replace it with a similar toy or find another type of toy that is appealing to the dog. But remember not to let the dog have the toy or one like it at any other time. This way the toy becomes the dog's special treat to look forward to and is reserved for times when you will be going out.

When you return and find that your dog has not been destructive, use positive reinforcement. Heap the dog with praise and reward and give it an extra-long run or play session.

When a dog's destructive behavior is confined to chewing, repellents may also help temporarily (see *Inappropriate Chewing, Biting, Mouthing, and Pica*, page 140) but the boredom that is at the root of the problem must be relieved at the same time. Otherwise, even the strongest repellent may cease to deter a frantic dog from destructive behavior.

15

Nine to Eleven Months: More Leveling Off

Just as there was a relatively calm period in your puppy's relationship with you when it was around four months old, these next two months are a generally stable time in most puppies' lives. It is the period before the final spurt into adulthood occurs for all but the very large and giant breeds of puppies. Small-breed puppies are just about as big as they will get, middle-sized puppies are almost full grown, while large and giant breeds still have a way to go. Even in those puppies that are still growing, the rate of growth is slowed appreciably, and you may notice that your puppy's frame is beginning to fill out. Some of the teenaged gangliness is replaced by a fuller, wider chest, and most puppies no longer seem to be all boney knees and big paws.

Table 23 HIGHLIGHTS CHART
Nine to Eleven Months: More Leveling Off

	PUPPY DEVELOPMENT		OWNER INVOLVEMENT	
	Physical	**Social/Behavioral**	**Puppy's Health/ Safety Needs**	**Working with Puppy Readiness**
Nine to Ten Months	Continues to grow and fill out Small breds are full grown	Generally stable Some puppies may continue to test and challenge authority‡ Destructive behavior may continue or recur	Feed two times/day† Protect unspayed females against accidental mating	Continue Positive Reinforcement*
			Increase exercise and play†	
			Regular grooming†	Don't allow Begging, Stealing Food*
Ten to Eleven Months	Possible first heat for large females Middle-sized dogs are almost full grown			Avoid "Negative Reinforcement"*

* *See Detailed Discussion.*   † See Chapter 4.   ‡ See Chapter 5.

230

A Quiet Time

As long as your puppy is getting sufficient exercise and activity, this is a fairly quiet time in its life. In general, your puppy is willing and anxious to learn. This is an excellent time to expand all of your training sessions at home and to begin teaching your puppy some new lessons. If your puppy has already mastered "basic training," this is a good time to teach it some tricks. Some puppies really enjoy the give-and-take of learning and are genuinely pleased with themselves when they master a new action; others are not particularly interested in learning tricks. You can gauge your own puppy's receptivity to learning tricks by its attention or lack of it and its reaction to the whole process. If your puppy loses interest quickly, it simply may not be old enough to concentrate on learning tricks yet. In this case, do not pursue it but try again when your puppy is a bit older. If you are in an obedience class, you may find that your puppy is attentive and eager to please within the structure of the class. If your puppy is one of the larger breeds, it will get increasingly strong physically, and you will be glad that you taught it proper leash manners when it was smaller.

Increased physical strength and stamina mean that your puppy needs even more and more frequent exercise and activity. With all but very delicate breeds, you do not have to worry anymore about overtiring your puppy with vigorous exercise or play. Children should be encouraged to include the puppy in their play and roughhouse sessions, within reason. Any vigorous activity is good for a puppy this age as long as it is not too prolonged or too strenuous. As your puppy continues to become stronger, this helps to offset destructive behavior that might otherwise continue to be a problem or could recur if you become lax or lazy about exercise.

Good Feeding Habits

Sufficient exercise also helps to keep your puppy trim and prevents excessive weight gain, but only if it goes hand in hand with good feeding habits. As your puppy grows and exercises more, it may seem to develop a tremendous appetite.

You need to feed your puppy enough every day to provide it with sufficient energy (calories) to maintain its strength and continue to grow and fill out, but this is the time to be careful not to overdo it because, in reality, even though your puppy may be larger, it does not need as many calories as it formerly did when it was growing so rapidly. Your puppy does not know enough to curb its intake when it has had enough, but will eat any food you offer it (and sometimes food you do not offer it—see below). Do not fall into the habit of constantly giving your puppy snacks or treats, and don't allow children or other family members to do so. By now you should have substituted praise and pats for food treats as rewards for good behavior. If not, now is the time to do so. Soon you may be cutting your puppy's feedings down to one a day, and the temptation to give it extra treats will be stronger.

This is especially important after your puppy has been neutered. Some male dogs seem to develop increased appetites immediately after castration, and it can be difficult not to overfeed them.

If you are in doubt as to how much to feed your puppy each day, talk it over with your veterinarian. A word of caution: Dog food manufacturers tend to overestimate dogs' caloric needs on package labels in order to assure proper nutrition and may recommend quantities of food that are too large for many dogs. Follow your veterinarian's advice about how much to feed your pet.

One bad habit that may arise around this time and is troublesome to a lot of dog owners is that of begging or even stealing food. It is very easy to prevent. All it usually takes is a lot of will power on your part and on that of your family and friends.

Begging and Stealing Food

Carol and John were entertaining Mr. and Mrs. Forbes, the owners of the bank that John had worked for for only six months. Anxious to make a good impression, they had worked all day Saturday shopping, cleaning the house, cooking and, in general, trying to create an atmosphere of a quiet, well-organized household. As the four of them sat at the candelit table and began to eat, Mrs. Forbes suddenly jumped and let out an exclamation. Looking under the table, John was horrified to see that Daisy, their two-year-old collie, had put her muzzle on Mrs. Forbes' lap and was standing, wagging her tail, waiting for a tidbit. He shooed the dog away with his napkin, but within minutes Daisy began to nuzzle Mr. Forbes. Disgusted, John got up, grabbed Daisy by the nape of the neck, and put her outside. She immediately set up a barking wail. John and Carol looked at each other in distress.

No dog that has not been properly taught not to beg at the table will know enough to put on "company manners" at will. You must realize that the canine behavior you and your family tolerate on an informal day-to-day basis can become very embarrassing when strangers are in your house.

As your puppy gets to the stage when it is allowed free run of your house most of the time, it may decide that it wants some of the delicious-smelling food on your table. Just one tiny bit of food, given unthinkingly by someone who "feels sorry" for a puppy that is looking wistful, can encourage any puppy to become a beggar.

It is important to be very strict about this: Never, ever feed a puppy anything while you are sitting and/or eating at the table, and do not allow other family members or visitors to do so. It doesn't matter whether you are having only a snack in the kitchen or a formal meal in the dining room. Your puppy does not know the difference. All it learns is that if it looks wistful, whines, barks, puts its head in your lap, or stands on its hind legs and puts its paws up, it may be fed a tasty morsel.

Some people opt to keep a puppy out of the dining room or kitchen altogether while they eat, either by closing it out with a gate or door, or by using verbal commands. We are opposed to the use of gates or doors because it places an unnecessary burden on you and teaches the puppy nothing. It is far better to take a little time and teach a puppy what you want with a verbal command such as "Go, settle," or show a puppy that you do not allow begging than to run around closing doors or gates every time you want to sit down at the table. Don't ever allow a puppy to wander around underfoot while food is being cooked and served; this can be dangerous.

If children or other softhearted family members feel they must, they can be allowed to take any leftover bit to the kitchen counter when they have finished eating, put it in the puppy's own feeding dish, and then let the puppy have it. A puppy should never be led to expect this after every meal, however. It will become overweight, and a habit will develop that you may not be prepared to follow through on each and every mealtime. Better yet, refrigerate any appropriate leftovers and add them later to your puppy's regular feeding. Then the puppy won't connect the special food with your mealtimes. Some owners find that it helps to feed a puppy its regular dinner meal just before the family eats theirs. This works if your family has a fairly regular mealtime schedule, but it won't help prevent begging at other times of the day.

If you begin teaching a puppy proper "table manners" early and consistently, your puppy will soon go to its place automatically whenever anyone sits down to eat, even for only a quick snack, and you need never be embarrassed to find your pet nuzzling a guest under the table.

STEALING FOOD

Some dogs seem to be hungry all the time, no matter how well fed. It is very tempting for these dogs to take mouth-watering food that is left unattended. A puppy must be taught never to help itself to any food that you don't give it, no matter how appealing it is.

Big dogs that can readily gain access to table and counter tops are more apt to be tempted to steal food in a kitchen or dining room, but little dogs can be very ingenious about jumping up on chairs or stools to reach food. Cocktail table snacks and outdoor picnics are very tantalizing (and accessible) for all dogs.

Most dogs do not try to steal food when people are around. If your puppy should make a move toward food, your immediate "No" and subsequent scolding should get the message across with no room for doubt.

Never allow a puppy to eat any food that it has stolen. Take it away immediately. If a puppy runs off with stolen food, go and get the puppy, take the food away, and bring the puppy back to the scene of the crime to scold it. It is very important to do this. Don't allow yourself to fall into an "it's ruined anyway, why not let the puppy enjoy it?" attitude. You would be teaching your puppy that it can not only get away with stealing food but is also allowed to savor its prize with no bad consequences.

If a puppy persists in stealing food when you are not around, you may have to resort to a set-up situation in which the animal punishes itself by its own actions. (This form of punishment is also described in *Inappropriate Chewing, Biting, Mouthing, and Pica*, page 140.) Saturate a tasty-looking morsel with something that tastes terrible, place it on a low table, and leave the room. When the puppy grabs the food it is immediately assailed with a horrid taste; it drops the food and probably won't attempt to steal food again—at least for some time.

Even when a puppy is well trained not to steal food, it is always a good idea to remind it with a "No" or "No take" if you are going to leave tempting food unattended in an easily accessible place for any length of time.

A Few Ripples

In addition to the possible recurrence of destructive behavior that we spoke of above, some puppies may suddenly decide that they are now grown up enough to challenge your authority. Feeling strong and fit and no longer completely dependent on you, a puppy that is naturally stubborn or strong willed may show some signs of testing you again, just as it did when it was a teenager. This tendency, which is stronger in some puppies than others, may continue for the next few months as the puppy nears maturity.

More Reinforcement

The minute you notice any rebellion or backsliding in appropriate behavior, whenever it occurs, bring out all your heavy artillery and stop it in its tracks, or you may be in for trouble. Your puppy is no longer a little baby, and you can't afford to let it get away with challenging you.

Reinforce and reinforce, and reteach and reteach, as often and as firmly as you can. Again, however, do not forget the power of praise. Your puppy still basically wants to please you, and positive reinforcement is one of your best weapons against rebellious behavior. Don't let your puppy begin to think it can gain your attention only by bad behavior. More about this and the undermining effects of unwittingly rewarding your puppy for bad behavior in the section on what we are calling *"Negative Reinforcement"* that follows.

Now that your puppy is no longer in danger of hurting itself accidentally and is completely housebroken, you have probably been allowing it to have the run of the house or at least part of the house most of the time. With this new freedom, new opportunities to form bad habits can easily occur. If misbehavior seems to be confined to one room of the house—getting up on the bed or sleeping on a couch in the den, for instance—the most effective deterrent when you are not going to be around is to close the door of the room in which the offense regularly occurs. This should be combined with appropriate verbal reinforcement when you are at home, however, or you may soon find that you are back to closing your puppy up in one room of the house when you go out. You probably do not want to go through the trouble of having to do this every day; in addition, this kind of incarceration is apt to add to your puppy's boredom which, as we have pointed out again and again, is the root of a number of behavior problems.

Remember, your puppy cannot read your mind. It interprets any actions on your part at face value. That is why you must be so careful not to give the wrong messages.

"Negative Reinforcement"

[Note: We are using the term "negative reinforcement" in this context to mean "the (often unconscious) reinforcement of unwanted or undesirable behavior." Scientifically, the term "negative reinforcement" means "the reinforcement of a behavior by removing an aversive stimulus"; in other words, an electric shock that is present when a dog nears a fence and is not activated when the dog does not go near the fence is a "negative reinforcer" that causes the animal to avoid the fence.]

The apartment doorbell rings and Fifi, a six-year-old Pomeranian, runs toward the front door yapping and growling hysterically. Her owner, Mrs. Jones, knowing from past experience that Fifi may nip the heels of whoever is outside, scoops up the little dog in her arms before opening the door. Holding the dog tightly, she murmurs, "No, no. Bad girl," and taps her lightly on the nose as Fifi continues to growl and yip at the visitor. The dog's aggressiveness seems to be getting worse, and Mrs. Jones attributes it to the fact that Fifi is getting older.

Phyllis and David have just sat down to dinner when their beagle, Josy, sets up a terrible baying and barking at the back door. Sighing resignedly, Phyllis gets up and lets Josy out the door. The dog races across the yard toward the fence, barking frantically at some unknown "intruder"—a squirrel, raccoon, or another dog, perhaps. Five minutes later, Josy is outside the door barking to come in. Less than ten minutes later, the barking resumes. This time David gets up to let Josy out and in again. This routine is repeated three more times before Phyllis and David can finally finish their dinner. "She's just trying to protect the house," they tell each other, but their patience is wearing thin.

These are both good examples of what we will call "negative reinforcement." In the first example Mrs. Jones has accomplished her purpose—to prevent her visitor from having nipped heels—but she has unconsciously made it more likely that the next visitor and the next and the next may not be so lucky. The message that Fifi is getting is that the more noise she makes and the more ferocious she is, the more attention she gets. If the truth be known, she has learned that the only time she is picked up and held very tightly by her favorite human is when she acts aggressively.

Mrs. Jones is completely unaware that she is actually rewarding Fifi for her bad behavior. Even her verbal scolding and the tap on the nose are welcome bits of attention to the dog. She usually allows the little dog to run around the apartment all day with little attention or affection except for an occasional pat. The same lack of attention can be felt by a dog living in an average household of people who are out at work or school all day. Like a child, Fifi is "acting up" to get attention, and succeeding.

Josy is doing the same thing by acting overly territorial. She is making sure that as soon as her humans sit down and pay no attention to her, her insistent barking will force them to react to her. Phyllis and David are also unconsciously encouraging her in her behavior. By jumping up and letting her out the minute she barks, they are giving her the message that her excessive territorial barking is a good way to get attention and create a little excitement at the same time. There is no way she can know that they are not enjoying the "game" as much as she is, since they play it so willingly.

Although both Fifi and Josy can probably be taught that their behavior is not acceptable, it will take time and effort to do so at this late date. It is far easier to avoid encouraging them in the first place!

In both instances, prompt action when these dogs were puppies could have demonstrated that certain

239

behaviors were *not* acceptable and would *not* be rewarded with favorable owner attention. (See also, *Discipline: Reward and Punishment*, page 93; *Positive Reinforcement*, page 213; *Nip Aggression in the Bud*, page 146; and *Excessive "Nuisance" Barking*, page 184.)

Eleven Months to a Year and a Half: Young Adulthood— Who's the Boss?

Sometime between eleven and eighteen months of age your puppy becomes a young adult. Physically and behaviorally it has pretty much become the adult dog that it will be from now on. Its frame will probably fill out some more, and it will calm down and become a bit more mellow in the next few years, but at the end of this period it is essentially grown up.

All but the very large and giant breeds are fully mature by the time they reach a year of age. Large breeds of dogs usually have achieved full physical growth by the time they are a year and a half old, and they have become behaviorally stable by two years of age. Giant breeds probably reach sexual maturity sometime during their second year but continue to grow in stature and weight until they are two or more years old. Their full behavioral maturity is delayed until they are two or more years of age.

This is a time when most puppies feel physically strong and emotionally secure. Although they certainly know most of your rules of behavior by now, many have enough

Table 24 HIGHLIGHTS CHART

Eleven Months to a Year and a Half: Young Adulthood—Who's the Boss?

	PUPPY DEVELOPMENT		OWNER INVOLVEMENT	
	Physical	**Social/Behavioral**	**Puppy's Health/ Safety Needs**	**Working with Puppy Readiness**
Eleven Months to One Year	Sexual maturity in all but giant breeds	May challenge authority again† Males may become overprotective and aggressive	Feed 2 meals/day† Protect unspayed females against accidental mating Regular grooming†	Continue to reinforce all previous lessons Control Mounting* in males Increase exercise and play†
One Year to Eighteen Months	Physical maturity— large dogs Giant breeds may reach puberty, first heat	Testing authority again‡	Annual checkup† Immunizations/ heartworm test† Feed one or two meals/ day§	Reinforce no Jumping Up on People* Firm hand needed Another Pet for Company?*

* See *Detailed Discussion*. † See Chapter 4. ‡ See Chapter 5. § See also *Time for a Health Check*, page 245.

242

self-confidence and bravado to see if they can get away with breaking a few of them.

Making Waves

Sometime between eleven months to one year of age, and again at about a year and a half, all but the most docile of puppies may put you to the test in one way or another. Sheer exuberance and good feelings can contribute in part to this seeming rebellion. Your young adult puppy may indulge in excessive wildness, running heedlessly away from you when you want to have a quiet game or obedience lesson, knocking things off table tops with its wildly wagging tail, and barking and jumping up on people. If this is the case, it's time for a calming down. Even if your puppy is a tiny toy breed, it's no fun to have a wildly careening animal around.

First, don't join in unstructured frantic play with your puppy. It may be a temptation for you or your children to get into the spirit when your older puppy begins to run around mindlessly, but just as this kind of undisciplined wild activity usually leads eventually to tears and hysterics when children are allowed to indulge in it, it can lead to chaos with a puppy and may be very hard to stop.

If your puppy shows signs of becoming overly wild or "silly" at this stage in its life, stop whatever activity you are engaged in with it. Sit down quietly and call the puppy to you. When it comes, pat and stroke it gently from head to toe and insist that it sit quietly, or put it in the "Down, stay" position and make it stay for at least fifteen minutes. When you release it, it is all right to continue to play, but insist that the puppy remain in the structure of the game. If you are playing "fetch," for instance, be sure that the puppy brings the object back to you each time and doesn't begin to run around with it. If your puppy starts to become overexcited and distracted again, stop the game once more and insist that the puppy stay quiet and calm for a longer period of time before you resume the activity. Wherever you are, repeat the same steps as many times as necessary until it quiets down.

It is possible that your overly exuberant puppy is not getting enough exercise and is feeling "hyper" because of this. This is especially true if it is a large, powerful, active breed of dog. It may have reached its full physical strength so quickly that you haven't kept up with its exercise needs. You should contrive to give it longer, more frequent walks and more ambitious runs if this is the case. We spoke of running or jogging with your puppy in Chapter 14. If this appeals to you as an appropriate way of exercising your puppy, all but the largest breeds are physically ready to begin this activity at about a year of age. Be sure to check with your veterinarian before you begin this or any other exercise routine.

Continue Reinforcement

Your puppy's testing at this time may not take the form of undisciplined activity but may simply consist of heedlessness or indifference to your wishes. As we have said throughout this book, never let your puppy get away with challenging your authority by pretending to forget or misunderstand familiar commands or by trying out some new form of inappropriate behavior. This is especially important at this time in your puppy's life when it is just entering adulthood. If you do not stop your young adult puppy in its tracks the minute it starts to misbehave, it may get the message that its new maturity and physical power have given it license to defy your authority.

Whether your puppy is eleven months old or over a year when it begins to challenge you, this is a crucial time for you to reassert your dominance by continuous reinforcement of appropriate behavior. Otherwise, your puppy will enter adulthood thinking it can lord it over you whenever it feels like it. If you allow this to happen, you will have to retrain your puppy all over again when it is an adult dog, and that will be a great deal more difficult than if you quickly remind it of its proper behavior now, while the memories of its not-so-distant dependent babyhood are still alive.

Of course, if yours is a very compliant, submissive puppy that always behaves and never makes waves, you may notice little of this late rebellion. Still, even the best-mannered puppy may test a little bit at this age, so be aware of the possibility. If you have an essentially angelic puppy that is completely tuned in to your wishes, you may need little more reinforcement than to say, "I'm surprised at you!" to squelch any incipient problem.

Time for a Health Check

When your puppy reaches its first birthday it is time for another visit to the veterinarian. At this time your puppy is given the first of its yearly immunization "boosters." From now on it should visit the veterinarian annually to be revaccinated against infectious diseases. The immunity that a dog receives in a vaccination does not last indefinitely, so annual revaccination (so-called booster shots) are necessary to ensure continued protection.

Depending on the type of vaccine used and the incidence of disease in the geographic area in which you live, your veterinarian may advise that some immunizations be given more frequently; others, such as rabies, are usually given at two- to three-year intervals. Always check with your veterinarian if you plan to take your puppy away with you; it may be advisable to have additional immunizations.

As we discussed in Chapter 4, a heartworm test should be given at least once a year in most geographic locations—more often in many.

This annual trip to the veterinarian for immunizations should also be the occasion for a physical checkup for your puppy. It is a good time to discuss with your veterinarian any concerns you may have about your puppy's well-being and an excellent opportunity for the doctor to assess your puppy's weight, exercise requirements, and so forth.

At about twelve months of age some puppies are ready to graduate to one meal per day. Large- or giant-breed puppies and those with special diet or digestive considerations may benefit from smaller, more frequent daily feedings throughout their lives, however. Some may continue to thrive on a self-feeding routine. Be sure to discuss feeding with your veterinarian who will know what type of feeding schedule generally works best for your particular type of dog. Remember that no puppy should ever indulge in vigorous exercise or play immediately after eating. This is particularly important for large and giant dogs that have a greater tendency to develop a potentially life-threatening condition known as "Bloat." Exercise after eating and drinking is known to be one causative factor of Bloat.

Sexual Maturity

By a year of age all but giant breeds of puppies have reached sexual maturity. Most of the giant breeds mature sexually by the time they are a year and a half old.

Coupled with increased physical power, sexual feelings may cause many male puppies to become overprotective of property and even of their owners. Naturally assertive males that indulged in sexually rooted aggressive behavior when they were eight or nine months old may again show a tendency to aggression in their roles as protectors. The difference between the potential for tragedy caused by aggressive behavior in an eight- or nine-month-old puppy and a fully-grown dog is marked, and you must be on your guard to stop any signs of aggression the minute that they begin. If necessary, reassert your dominance over your puppy (see *Nip Aggression in the Bud*, page 146). It may not be easy to do with a large puppy, but you have to do it now, before your puppy thinks that it can get away with bullying you.

You may also need to reinforce other good behaviors that you thought were part of your dog's basic nature by now. Territorial "nuisance" barking may resurface, as well as inter-dog aggression. Even sexual urine marking may very well occur, especially if your puppy has not yet been neutered. All of these behaviors are completely "natural" for a sexually active, vigorous dog, but you have to remind your pet that they are not behaviors you will permit.

Although it is not generally a sexually oriented behavior, jumping up on people may become more of a problem as your puppy gets bigger, and even though it usually begins out of exuberance, it can develop into a sexual act, especially with large males. It should be stopped right away if it occurs.

Left unchecked, jumping up can easily turn into mounting behavior.

Mounting in Male Dogs

Six-year-old Linda was strolling up her front walk with her friend Polly when the family's four-year-old Great Pyrenees, Prince, came to greet them. She petted the big dog's head and put her arms around his neck, and Polly followed suit. Suddenly, Prince began to nudge Polly rather hard. Giggling, she moved away, and Prince stood up on his hind legs and put his front paws on her shoulders. Still giggling, she tried to back off, but Prince persisted and succeeded in pushing her down on the grass on her back. He began to straddle her while she lay terrified. Linda ran into the house screaming for her mother.

Marcia was sitting in her living room with two very proper ladies who had come to interview her for membership in the local country club. She had just served them tea in her best china and was making polite conversation. As she spoke, she was horrified to see that Max, her two-year-old dachshund, was sniffing one of the lady's crossed legs. Before she could stop him he had wrapped his short front legs around the lady's calf and begun to "hump" her leg.

Mounting can be a source of embarrassment when your dog is small, but it can be frightening and dangerous if you have a large breed such as Prince.

Puppies often mount littermates in play, and both male and female puppies sometimes mount other household pets as a show of dominance. Some puppies even take to mounting inanimate objects—sofa cushions, blankets, even chair legs. Immediate, consistent intervention is effective in stopping this before it becomes a habit. Clap your hands, say "No" firmly, and remove the puppy from its "victim" each time mounting behavior begins.

In a mature male dog, mounting is usually sexual in nature. Early castration as a puppy, before mounting becomes a habit, is the best way to prevent this kind of problem from developing later on. Large- and giant-breed dogs that reach sexual maturity late often don't exhibit mounting behavior until they are three or four years old, and then it may occur suddenly with no warning. Sometimes it is exacerbated when a nearby female dog is in heat. Castration at this time is relatively effective, but it is much more foolproof when performed before the behavior develops.

We discuss other types of sexual behavior, such as roaming, urine marking, aggression, and so forth, in *Castration (Neutering, Altering)* on page 214.

Social Interaction

Your puppy's relationship to you, the rest of your family, and other familiar people is fairly well established by the time it reaches eleven months of age. Although you may surprise it by taking it to new places—on vacation with you or to a new park to run, for example—its physical world is probably quite circumscribed in general. At this stage in your young adult dog's life there are few major surprises. No wonder it feels the urge to stir things up once in a while by acting in an unpredictable way or by roaming a few blocks! If it becomes bored enough as time goes on, you may find that other behavior problems suddenly rear their unpleasant heads.

Before your pet becomes too set in its ways, be sure that it is able to accept your absence. If you or other family members are routinely at home most of the time, make a point of leaving your puppy alone in the house once in a while before it becomes too dependent on your presence (see *Helping a Puppy Learn to Tolerate Human Absence*, page 173). At this time in its life it is also a good idea to leave it for a day or overnight in a boarding kennel if you have not done so for some time, in order to reinforce its ability to accept a stay away from familiar territory and people without suffering undue trauma. In *Learning to Stay Away from Home*, page 207, we discuss the reasons for this and the way in which to go about it.

As your puppy grows up and out of dependent baby-hood and becomes a self-sufficient adult dog it is very easy to forget that it still needs love, companionship, praise, and entertainment. You have taken it away from its mother and littermates and have gone to some pains to impress upon this puppy that you are its pack leader. Now that it no longer requires physical care from you as frequently and is generally well established as far as proper behavior goes, it is easy to fall into the habit of taking it for granted most of the time.

If you find that you are spending less and less time with your young adult puppy, you may feel concerned that it might become bored and lonely. Your own social and business obligations can often come in the way of spending as much time together as either you or your puppy would like. Before you start to feel guilty and your puppy begins to feel the need to gain your attention by misbehaving, you may want to consider getting another pet to keep it company. Even if you did not originally think about adopting two puppies, this may be the time to give the idea serious thought. It may be the best gift that you can give your young adult puppy and yourself, and be the final step in bringing up your puppy to be a truly wonderful adult dog.

Another Pet for Company?

Fred and Mary both work fairly long hours. Pierre, their standard poodle, seemed to have learned to accept their daily absences calmly until he was almost full grown, at about a year of age. Then they often began to find that he had knocked over the wastebaskets and pulled the chair cushions down onto the floor during the day. When scolded, he was very contrite, but as time went on he became more and more destructive in their absence. Soon he was not only knocking things down but chewing on them. Today, when they returned from work tired and hungry after a long day, they discovered that Pierre had not only completely destroyed a needlepoint cushion that Mary's mother had made for them but had created a terrible mess as well, strewing pieces of the cushion all over the house. They are at their wits' end and are seriously considering giving Pierre away, even though he is a wonderful dog in every other way.

Pierre is not only bored he also gets lonely and full of pent-up energy when left alone for eight or more hours. As we discussed before, dogs are social animals and require a lot of company. Young, barely adult dogs that have reached physical maturity are particularly apt to begin to misbehave when they become physically restless after a long period of time, especially when this occurs day after day. With nothing better to do, many dogs revert to "babyish" habits; they may chew and wet, bark continuously, knock things over, or engage in other types of destructive behavior. Other dogs become depressed, moody, or develop neuroses, phobias, or other personality quirks.

Although a second pet cannot take the place of human company, it usually helps prevent or diminish behavior problems when they are due to boredom, restlessness, and loneliness during owners' absences.

LOSS OF A PUPPY'S AFFECTION?

Many people are seriously concerned that if they adopt two pets at the same time, the animals will become more devoted to each other than to them. Or if they already have a dog, they worry that by getting another puppy (or a kitten) they will forfeit their puppy's companionship and affection. Our answer is that this simply is not true. What happens when you get a companion for your pet is that you gain the affection and companionship of two pets instead of one.

When a second puppy or kitten is introduced into

251

your household (see *Introducing a New Pet to an Older Dog*, page 254) your existing puppy is still your friend and companion, but you are relieved of the burden of entertaining it and providing it with company all the time. You no longer need to feel guilty if work or play keeps you away from home longer than usual, and your puppy is not as lonely and bored when you're not there.

When raising two puppies at the same time, whether or not from the same litter, you need to be careful that they don't become too dependent on each other to the exclusion of everyone else. Not only does this kind of interdependence interfere with your relationship with each of your pets but it also leads to terrible stress for the dogs should they ever have to be separated later in life. This is not difficult to do but entails giving each puppy individual experiences, time away from its companion, and time alone with you and other family members. Leave one puppy home when you take the other for a walk or run or ride in the car. Leave one dog indoors while the other romps with you or another person in the yard, and so forth. Do this regularly, and be sure that each puppy gets equal time in equal activities. Each puppy then grows up able to function independently of the other in a variety of situations and relationships.

WHAT KIND OF COMPANION PET?

Although another dog may seem the obvious answer as a companion for a puppy, many owners simply do not want two dogs or do not have space for them. We have found that a puppy and a kitten are ideal companion pets. Even a very young kitten requires a good deal less physical care and owner attention than a young puppy does, and cats take up very little space. A kitten should remain primarily an indoor cat, however, because if it is allowed out all day to roam around, it will not provide much company for a housebound puppy.

If you are anticipating getting two puppies, they should be opposite sexes. (The sex of a cat is not a factor.) Of course, neutering and/or spaying of both cats and dogs is strongly recommended for both physical and behavioral benefits, no matter what the combination of sexes.

Two puppies from the same litter are ideal companions as long as they have independent experiences once they are adopted. By the time they are adopted, they already have developed their dominant/submissive roles, which is fine because it eliminates the need to establish who is "top dog" later on.

When you already have a dog and are getting a second, it is always best to choose a puppy that is younger than yours. An older dog (even one that is barely grown) almost always accepts a young puppy more easily than a dog that is the same age or older. When a younger pet is brought into a household with a resident older dog, use common sense in its selection. Although opposites in temperament often get along well, you want to avoid obvious physical peril to either animal, and you don't want either to feel bullied or threatened. If your puppy is extremely shy and somewhat timid, it would be best to avoid an overly aggressive, boisterous, new puppy. However, since you want to avoid having two timid puppies, do get one that is somewhat assertive so that it will give added confidence to your timid puppy. On the other hand, if you have a very energetic, physically active puppy that likes to chase squirrels in the yard, perhaps an equally active puppy, or a competent (primarily indoor) older cat is the answer. Size should also be a factor. Obviously, a tiny kitten is in some danger from a Great Dane, no matter how gentle the dog may be. And if you have a delicate toy poodle, a big strong Labrador retriever puppy may be too much for it to handle.

INTRODUCING A NEW PET TO AN OLDER DOG

Before bringing any new pet into your household, both animals should have up-to-date immunizations and veterinary examinations to be sure they are in good general health. This is not only to protect against the spread of parasites and infection but also to make sure they both feel well. Even minor illnesses and infections can make an animal crabby and less apt to be tolerant of others.

A serious drawback to waiting until a dog is grown or almost mature before introducing a new pet into the household is that the dog's territorial instincts are usually fully developed. This instinct is stronger in some dogs than others and is apt to be more pronounced in males than in females.

No matter what kind of companion pet is chosen, you should anticipate some initial resentment or at least wariness. To avoid problems, the introduction requires some advance thought and planning, and should be gradual. It is foolish to think that Pierre, who has ruled the roost until now, will automatically welcome Rover or Felix into *his* home with equanimity.

To ease the introduction, bring the two animals together for the first time on neutral ground, away from home territory. They can meet in a park or field if the newcomer is another puppy, or in a neighbor's yard or living room if it's a kitten. That way Pierre can sniff and explore the newcomer for a while without feeling that his home is being invaded and threatened. The newcomer won't be frightened and defensive, and the two can become acquainted quietly. After the animals have spent some time together they can be taken home.

This system does not necessarily avoid all problems of territoriality and jealousy. No matter how well they seem to get along when someone is at home, the two animals should not be left alone together until you are sure they won't hurt each other. Surprisingly, however, fighting often only occurs in the presence of owners. If this happens, you should examine your own behavior to find out what you are doing to trigger aggression or jealousy.

The original pet's possessions and favorite playthings should be strictly off-limits to the newcomers, and if either animal needs to be confined, it should be the new one. If the new pet is a kitten or a small puppy, a simple tension gate across a door is an excellent way to keep it safely confined, away from the older animal's food and bed; at the same time this provides an opportunity for the two animals to gradually get used to each other's sight, smell, and sounds.

Most dogs accept a puppy or kitten very well, but some of the larger, exuberant breeds must learn to be gentle. After they develop muscular control, kittens can usually get out of the way when they need to and can use their claws to signal "enough," but little puppies must be protected from larger dogs until they are sure on their feet.

Even if the animals never become inseparable friends, the very presence of another pet in the house generally provides enough stimulation and companionship for a dog to help offset severe problems of loneliness, boredom, and misdirected energy.

Occasional Backsliding

Once you have overcome any latent rebellion that may have occurred in your puppy's final spurt toward adulthood, life with your now-grown young dog should be pretty smooth.

From this time on, however, there are some dogs that seem to backslide occasionally and require some reminding of proper behavior. If your dog was well trained as a puppy, immediate reinforcement usually does the trick.

If your dog has been neutered, sexually based problems such as aggression, roaming, and excessive territoriality do not usually occur once the dog matures, if it has been properly handled as a puppy. However, changed circumstances can sometimes cause a formerly well-behaved dog to forget or ignore lessons that were learned in the past.

A move to another home, the sudden absence of a favorite human or companion pet, illness, or a lengthy stay in a kennel can cause an adult dog to suffer from anxiety, which in turn can create behavior problems. These problems can usually be solved with patience, understanding, and consistent reinforcement. Sometimes, however, a dog may need to be completely retrained. You may have to begin all over again to teach your dog errorless housebreaking, for example, or start from scratch to prevent it from indulging in inappropriate chewing. If you have established a good relationship with your pet as a puppy, this should not be too difficult or take a very long time.

It is possible for you to be too close to a problem with your dog or too emotionally involved to see the cause of a behavior problem objectively and be able to determine a solution. If a behavior problem with your dog becomes serious and you are unable to solve it, an animal behaviorist may be of help.

Conclusion

As your dog ages and continues to mature, it may surprise you from time to time by its seeming awareness of your feelings and needs. In turn, you will find that you understand more and more about your dog's personality and the idiosyncrasies that make it unique. This bonding is what good dog ownership is all about. Yours is now a wonderful, companionable dog because you have been a caring, responsible owner.

INDEX

* Each bold-faced entry is a self-contained, in-depth Detailed Discussion of one aspect of puppy management or behavior that may be applicable at many stages of a puppy's life. For easy reference, each discussion is set off by a bold line in the left-hand margin of the text.

Index

Index

About the Author

Elizabeth Randolph is the pet care editor for *Family Circle* magazine and the author of numerous books and articles about pets and pet health. She lives in Mamaroneck, New York.

511

CPSIA information can be obtained
at www.ICGtesting.com
Printed in the USA
LVOW12s1632160517
534727LV00001B/177/P